: landscape london

a guide to recent parks, gardens and urban sp

landscape london

ellipsis

charlotte hare
photographs by maria satur

a guide to recent parks, gardens and urban spaces

A CIP record for this book is available from the British Library

PUBLISHED BY •••ellipsis
2 Rufus Street London N1 6PE
E MAIL ...@ellipsis.co.uk
WWW http://www.ellipsis.com
SERIES EDITOR Tom Neville
EDITOR Rosa Ainley

COPYRIGHT © 2001 Ellipsis London Limited
ISBN 1 84166 028 0

PRINTING AND BINDING Hong Kong

•••ellipsis is a trademark of Ellipsis
London Limited

For a copy of the Ellipsis catalogue or
information on special quantity orders
of Ellipsis books please contact
us on 020 7739 3157 or sales@ellipsis.co.uk

•••

landscape london: a guide to recent gardens, parks and urban spaces

Introduction

The character of London is the sum of its parts – including its buildings, roads, and waterways – but it is particularly famous for its landscape gardens and parks, and its abundance of trees. Unlike continental capitals such as Paris, London was never planned on a grand scale. Historically subdivided between Westminster, the seat of political control, and the City, the centre of commerce, the two have merged and spread outwards, absorbing one village after another.

Most history books will tell you that the 'public park' – an area of open land laid out for the public to enjoy within a built-up area – was invented in Britain, towards the middle of the nineteenth century. In fact, London's first public park, Finsbury Circus, was laid out in 1606. The royal parks, such as St James's Park, Greenwich Park and Richmond Park, were laid out following the restoration of Charles II to the English throne in 1660, after his 13 years of exile in France. In search of opportunities to assert his regal mastery, he employed (among others) André le Nôtre, Louis XIV's garden designer at Versailles, to transform formerly enclosed areas of forest dedicated to the hunting pursuits of the court with grand avenues and paths into settings suitable for royal pageants. In 1666, the devastation wreaked by the Fire of London led to the first attempt to plan the reconstruction of the City of London, masterminded by Sir Christopher Wren.

A number of London's public parks and gardens were originally the ornamental grounds of large town houses. These include Holland Park, Gunnersbury Park and Chiswick House, laid out in the eighteenth and nineteenth centuries. After the Second World War, changes in lifestyles and steep inheritance duties led many landowners to relinquish their houses and grounds to the public domain.

The majority of London squares were laid out as part of housing developments built by astute landowners, perhaps most notably Lord Gros-

contents

venor. In the early nineteenth century the plans of John Nash, architect to the Crown, for Regent's Park show more than 30 houses in a landscaped setting as part of an idea for a smart London suburb. The concept was only partially realised.

The nineteenth-century public parks, such as Battersea Park, Crystal Palace Park and Victoria Park, were conceived as oases of clean air providing relief from the pollution generated by the industrial revolution. Their establishment carried underlying social messages promoting education, social and moral improvement.

As London's urban mass grew and increased in density, so the notion of an integrated system of linked open spaces (designed or otherwise) evolved. In the 1940s Lord Abercrombie saw the potential for developing the vast areas devastated by bombing in the Second World War. Drawing on earlier strategies, his vision involved creating a series of 'green lungs' linking central London to the green belt (instituted in 1929). Large areas of such land have since been designated Metropolitan Open Space and protected from development, such as Mile End Park and Burgess Park, but the full extent of Abercrombie's vision has never been realised.

In the 1980s many of London's derelict industrial sites were given a new lease of life, particularly the docks on either side of the river Thames between Tower Bridge and the Isle of Dogs, now known as Docklands. Predominantly funded by the private sector, the motives were commercial and Docklands was consequently crammed with expensive housing and offices – only a fraction of the area was given over to public open space.

The 1980s also saw the rise of the business park, of which Stockley Park (see page 1.10) is perhaps the most famous. Canary Wharf, its successor, is essentially an urban business park. Its designation as an Enterprise Zone meant relaxed planning standards to entice developers.

a guide to recent parks, gardens and urban spaces

Here developers saw the value in creating pleasant external environments for office workers. Tall office buildings are grouped around a series of piazzas, squares and courtyards, linked by a linear boulevard that permits vehicle access almost everywhere. The masterplan is in its final phase but Canada Square (see page 6.12) is the first area of open green space to date.

This is the perfect time to look at London's most recently designed (public) parks, gardens and urban spaces. The portfolio covers a much wider spectrum than ten years ago, proof that this area of design is in a period of experimentation and purposefulness. This is partly due to the varied sources of funding, such as EC grants, the government's Single Regeneration Budget (SRB), not forgetting the Lottery Commission. It also partly stems from changes in attitude – landscape and urban design are now more integral parts of the planning process. There is too a growing interest in design generally, and a greater concern for the environment. For example, the extension of Docklands eastwards beyond the Isle of Dogs/Greenwich Peninsula already includes two new public parks, Thames Barrier Park (more than 9.4 hectares) and Royal Arsenal Gardens (2.7 hectares). These parks are intended to act as catalysts, to stimulate urban regeneration in advance of any built development. The intent is still commercial but the approach is much more public-spirited.

An integrated park system seems to be back on the agenda once more. Over the last ten years there have been numerous strategies for London. In particular, the Thames Landscape Strategy has received wide recognition. Prepared by Kim Wilkie Associates, the report provides a 100-year strategy for the Thames Riverside between Hampton and Kew and there are plans to extend the strategy eastwards. With the recent election of the mayor and London Assembly, London will soon be the beneficiary of a city-wide Spatial Development Strategy (SDS). It is to be hoped that this will embrace some of the landscape strategies and studies that have focused on different areas and aspects of London in recent history.

The last few years of the twentieth century saw a flurry of landscape activity. The first batch of lottery projects, in particular those funded by the Millennium Commission, is only just complete. A major failing of many of the lottery projects so far is the lack of thought given to the maintenance of new or regenerated spaces. This has been recognised in the form of the New Opportunities Fund (set up to replace the Heritage Lottery Fund) which has a green space initiative aimed at long-term management of public open space.

International competitions have attracted designers from abroad, bringing freshness and new ideas, which should be examined and understood. For example, the French landscape profession is less used to overseeing the detailing and implementation of landscape schemes. In most instances this role has been fulfilled by UK landscape architects. To me it is an equally important, if not the most difficult, part of the whole process. There is a very distinct American flavour – characterised by polished pink granite – to many recent commercial schemes, and this may not always be appropriate. Finally, there's a timely wake-up call for the landscape profession – several of the major lottery-funded projects were masterplanned by architects.

The future looks even brighter. A number of schemes missed my deadlines but will be open to the public by the time this book is published. See, in particular, Royal Victoria Square at the entrance to the new Exhibition Centre on Royal Victoria Dock, E16. Designed by EDAW/Patel Taylor Architects/Aspen Burrow Crocker, it should add a pearl to the string in this up-and-coming area. Another lottery-funded project, Waltham Abbey Royal Gunpowder Mills, will open (in part) to the public

a guide to recent parks, gardens and urban spaces

Introduction

at easter 2001. A former Ministry of Defence site decommissioned in 1991, the 71-hectare site is extremely complex. Pearson Landscape Design, among others, have worked hard to create an interpretative site rather than a museum.

A number of foreign practices are notably absent from the book. They include Gustafson Porter (Crystal Palace Park, SE26 and Swiss Cottage Library, NW3) and Max Gross (Hackney Town Hall, E8; St John's Square, EC1; Islington Green, N1). Their respective schemes should be completed over the next few years and are worth looking out for. Following the decision to enlarge the size of Jubilee Gardens in Rick Mather's masterplan for the South Bank, the scheme by the Rotterdam practice, West 8 can no longer be directly used. Some schemes to look forward to from UK landscape architects include: Shoreditch Park, N1; Regent's Place, Euston Road, NW1 (Edwards Gale); Duke of York Headquarters, SW1 (Elizabeth Banks Associates); 1 Westminster Bridge, SW1 (J & L Gibbons); and Southwark Park, SE1 (Land Use Consultants).

On a larger scale, Artscape 13 aims to improve the visual experience for residents, pedestrians and road users along a 3-mile stretch (between Movers Lane and the new junction with the A1306) of east London's busiest arterial road, the A13. This will include designs for Goresbrook and Newlands Park, and some unusual ideas for lighting. The World Squares initiative, masterplanned by Foster and Partners, focuses on Whitehall, the ceremonial route connecting Parliament Square and Trafalgar Square and its environs. Without going down the road of mass pedestrianisation, it aims to redress the balance between pedestrian and car; to make visiting London's significant visitor attractions a more pleasurable experience; to reinforce the historic connections between buildings and open spaces; to encourage Londoners to use their squares and more people to travel on foot. Improvements to Old Palace Yard by Civic Design Partnership should also be under way (see also Horse Guards, page 3.22)

Most of the schemes in this book, chosen from some 200 visited, have been publicised in professional journals and gardening magazines, or suggested to me by designers. They are the work of fellow professionals: architects, urban designers, garden designers, even whole communities. All were completed in the last ten years. The schemes are grouped by borough and most are in inner London, easily accessible by public transport and visitors don't need to book in advance.

BIBLIOGRAPHY
I have consulted the following books and magazines in putting this book together; any of them would be useful for further reading purposes.
Samantha Hardingham, *London: a guide to recent architecture*, Ellipsis, 1999; *Green Spaces Guide to London 1999*, Verdant Books, 1999; *The Good Gardens Guide*, Bloomsbury, 1999.
The Architects' Journal; *Building Design*; *Gardens Illustrated*; *Guardian, Space*; *Homes and Property, Evening Standard*; *Landscape Design*; *Time Out*; *The London Gardener* (Journal of the London Parks and Gardens Trust).

ACKNOWLEDGEMENTS
Many thanks to everyone who helped and inspired me to put this guide together. I hope that it will encourage debate and criticism.

hillingdon to hammersmith & fulham

British Airways (Waterside) at Harmondsworth Moor

The payoff for BA's new headquarters (by Neils Thorp with Renton Howard Wood Levin (RHWL) Partnership) in London's green belt is the reclamation as public parkland of a much larger area of contaminated land known as Harmondsworth Moor. Land Use Consultants (LUC) claim it's the largest area of public open space created in London in the twentieth century. It has been widely acclaimed.

The whole site had been used for gravel extraction and refuse filling. LUC resolved to deal with the landfill problem on site. Refuse was sculpted into mounds, sealed with clay and covered by soil, creating acoustic and visual barriers. The processes, products and after-use are all in line with the post-1992 Rio environmental agenda. Major roads like the M25 and M4 dissect the site, effectively creating 12 separate plots, linked by an extensive gravel-path system. The gravels were dug from the site and topped with self-binding gravel from Oxfordshire. Paths are used to exaggerate landform and give the widest range of experience to walkers. Customised site furniture of fences, seats, way markers and signs avoids the suburbanisation of the country without adopting a rustic look.

The rivers were corridors of vitality: clear, chalk-fed and of high ecological and landscape value. Seventy-five thousand trees and scrub stock were planted small, augmented by tree seeding. Moor and heathland grass species were sown to create a more shaggy appearance than that given by the usual amenity mixes. Some areas were sown with seed from donor ancient meadow sites with matching characteristics. Existing trees, hedges, and river margins, protected during construction, are now correctly managed, bringing a more loved feel to this urban-fringe area.

BA's smart headquarters cover approximately 12 per cent of the site, set within tamed parkland. There are formal reflecting pools, fountains,

Land Use Consultants 1991

British Airways (Waterside) at Harmondsworth Moor

Land Use Consultants 1991

British Airways (Waterside) at Harmondsworth Moor

a massive boulder beach, stone causeway and lawns. Six U-shaped buildings are linked by a 175-metre-long atrium nicknamed 'The Street', a focal point with cafés, shops and seating. The internal landscape works both ways, drawing the surrounding landscape into the building using paving, water, trees (3- and 7-metre-high black olives and Cuban figs) and artwork, with extensive views through walls of panelled glass.

Each building overlooks a courtyard garden. Constructed as roof gardens over basement parking, significant technical constraints such as limited soil depth, drainage, and deep shade had to be accommodated. Each garden is designed to evoke the spirit of a continent, more apparent in some gardens than others. Perhaps the most successful one is Northern Europe with its 'ferns, foxgloves and silver birch'. Ironically, Africa is given the least space, with terracotta and blue brickwork with phormium and fatsia plants in giant pots.

Art in the landscape is low-key but includes works by artists such as Andy Goldsworthy. One site acquired by BA contained worked stone from Waterloo Bridge, which has since been recycled to make a skyline viewing point.

ADDRESS Harmondsworth Moor, Middlesex
CLIENT British Airways PLC
CONTRACT VALUE £4 million (external parkland); £4 million (courtyard and building); £35 million (land purchase, groundworks)
SIZE 110 hectares
TUBE Hatton Cross
RAIL West Drayton
ACCESS parkland area open; BA's offices by appointment only

Land Use Consultants 1991

British Airways (Waterside) at Harmondsworth Moor

Land Use Consultants 1991

Bedfont Lakes

Bedfont Lakes is a country park situated in the green belt. From the late 1800s until the 1920s the site formed part of a large orchard that supplied fruit to Covent Garden Market. Like many sites to the west of London, it was worked for sand and gravel until the 1960s. Three gravel pits, straddling the London to Windsor railway line at East Bedfont, were abandoned and used as a refuse tip. This ceased in 1973, leaving a mixture of polluted lakes, contaminated wasteland and derelict buildings.

Following a public inquiry in 1988, Hounslow Borough Council granted permission for office developments on part of the site (which now include IBM offices designed by Michael Hopkins and Partners), with a proviso that the wider area should be cleaned up for the benefit of the general public.

The series of hills along the southern boundary was formed by piling up 2 million cubic metres of soil and refuse – equivalent to 100,000 lorry loads. These were capped with clay and soil and then seeded with a wildflower mix. One of the hills, Millennium Monolith, is the highest point in the borough of Hounslow. The existing lakes were extended to the north. Paths hug the edges of three open spaces, winding in and out of the hillocks. Unobtrusive fencing protects the new native woodland and an area proudly proclaimed by a sign to be the 'richest wildflower meadows in London'. It is a rapidly maturing and attractive landscape where wildlife and potentially conflicting leisure pursuits seem to coexist harmoniously.

The project also provided a much-needed local relief link at Bedfont Road, giving access to the New Square and Clockhouse Place developments. Close to Stockley Park and both business parks, it is worth comparing the two schemes. Stockley Park is essentially a product of the 1980s, while Bedfont Lakes is firmly of the 1990s. At Bedfont, less

Bedfont Lakes

conventional landscape operations have been adopted; these include tree seeding under crops of winter wheat and barley, and the reintroduction of earthwork plots to increase worm activity, and frogs and toads to ponds. The community has been much more involved, with local children even planting acorns and small trees. Both developments involved re-excavation of landfill at an early stage to provide a clean building platform, with excavated waste being deposited in the landscape areas.

ADDRESS Clockhouse Lane, Bedfont, Hounslow, Middlesex
CLIENT Hanover Property Unit Trust (formerly Rutland Project Management Ltd)
ENGINEER Rust Environmental Ltd
CONTRACT VALUE £25 million
MAINTENANCE COSTS £160,000 a year (£1.95 million negotiated as contribution in perpetuity for maintenance)
SIZE 100 hectares
TUBE Heathrow Terminal 4, short bus or taxi ride
RAIL Ashford, then 1-mile walk or bus ride
ACCESS open 8.00 until dusk, except Christmas Day

Land Use Consultants 1995

Bedfont Lakes

Land Use Consultants 1995

Stockley Park

Stockley Park remains Britain's most famous business park. Situated opposite Heathrow and next to the M4, it's a commercial location to die for. The original aspiration, as defined by British developer Stuart Lipton, was all about PhDs rolling in the grass.

The business-park concept is imported from north America. Its roots can be traced to Silicon Valley, California, in the 1960s. It has been described as a descendant of the twentieth-century industrial-estate and garden-city movements, combining the experience of garden festivals with the future-city thinking of international expos. It has come to represent one of the most ambitious exercises of instant landscape (vast earth moving, lake making and planting) on a scale not seen in landscape design since the eighteenth-century English Landscape Garden movement.

The Arup Associates masterplan includes high-quality management and good security cover. The coherent and extendable layout is respectful of its green-belt context and provides flexibility both inside and outside the buildings. These are arranged as a series of pavilions, as integral to the landscape as eighteenth-century follies.

The character and speed of implementation of each phase will continue to depend on the economic health of the country. Phase 1 works involved cleaning up a 160-hectare rubbish tip: removing hazardous gas and groundwater pollution; scooping out 11 lakes; planting 170,000 trees and shrubs to encourage wildlife; building the business park and providing a public park for the borough of Hillingdon, including a golf course. All that between 1984 and 1990!

Phase 2, known as The Square, is situated to the west of phase 1 and is completely different in character. The land parcel is much smaller with six buildings (most designed by Arup) squeezed inside. An avenue of lime trees known as the 'necklace' snakes its way from east to west, linking

Arup Assocs/Bernard Ede/Charles Funke Assocs 1984–2001

Arup Assocs/Bernard Ede/Charles Funke Assocs 1984–2001

it to phase 1. The external spaces are treated more formally. The buildings are organised around a central area planted with circles of Atlas cedars (*Cedrus atlantica*). Swathes of box, juniper and a low-growing pyracantha (*Pyracantha koidzumii* 'Red Cushion') are intermittently broken up with lawn. The successful tall hedges around the car parks in phase 1 are repeated.

Stockley Park's success in landscape terms is due to good masterplanning and foresight. There has been a maintenance base on site since the beginning with the same contractor involved for more than ten years.

Phase 3 is yet to be completed. Let's hope that by the time it happens the long overdue provision of good public transport has been addressed.

ADDRESS Stockley Park, Uxbridge, Middlesex
CLIENT Stockley Park Consortium Ltd
RECLAMATION CONSULTANTS Grontmij NV/LRDC International Ltd
GOLF-COURSE CONSULTANTS Robert Trent Jones
CONTRACT VALUE £22 million, land engineering, reclamation and landscape works; £5 million, open spaces
SIZE 16 hectares
RAIL Uxbridge, then short bus ride
ACCESS open

Arup Assocs/Bernard Ede/Charles Funke Assocs 1984–2001

Arup Assocs/Bernard Ede/Charles Funke Assocs 1984–2001

Heathrow Airport Entrance

Concord Roundabout is the main approach to terminals 1, 2 and 3 at Heathrow airport. New three-tier walls on either side of the Nimrod bridge smarten up the entrance to the tunnel and conceal 800 new car-parking spaces behind the west retaining wall.

At such a busy junction, construction was never going to be simple. The solution combines concrete blocks, reinforced earth and soil nails. The sculpted walls are dressed in bands of different coloured blocks with diode lighting (by DPA and Peter Fink) reminiscent of runways. The hard lines of the walls are softened by a line of boxed lime trees silhouetted against the skyline, wrapped and retained by bands of beech hedging and smart galvanised railings.

It's an impressive new gateway to Heathrow and a classy stage for advertising boards, but, logically speaking, it's on the wrong side. First-time visitors to the UK will only be aware of this 'gateway' on their return to the airport. Perhaps last impressions are just as important. It's also a hard place to visit as the roundabout makes it a difficult place to stop. So this is one to look out for when you are on your way somewhere abroad – particularly at night.

ADDRESS Heathrow Airport, Northern Perimeter Road
CLIENT British Airways Association
CIVIL ENGINEERING DESIGN TPS Consulting
CONTRACT VALUE £7.5 million
TUBE Heathrow Terminals 1, 2 and 3
ACCESS open

TBV Consult/HED/EDAW 1997

hillingdon to hammersmith & fulham

Kew Public Record Office

The Public Record Office (PRO) houses the original records of the UK government dating back to the Domesday Book in 1086. It's also responsible for conserving the records of modern governmental departments and public bodies (since the late eighteenth century) and earlier records including those of the Admiralty, the War Office, the Board of Trade, the Colonial Office and the Treasury. It has an extensive map, photographic and flag archive too.

The 1977 PRO building has been refurbished and extended. The character of the extension is deliberately in contrast to the older building. The low roof line, the abundance of windows and the new pocket-park are much more in keeping with the public-spirited role and status of the institution. The neighbourhood population, anxious about yet another building programme in their locale, won the right to use the park as a planning gain.

Buildings now occupy 50 per cent of the total site. An adjacent railway embankment, terrace housing and the nearby Inland Revenue building restrict views and the pocket-park could potentially feel claustrophobic. The reflective qualities of the new series of water gardens seem to be the key here. They also creatively solve the problems of surface-water run-off and flood control which is necessary due to the proximity of the Thames. New vehicle access, service roads, staff and public parking are pushed against the boundary. There are new entrance gates and railings designed by Alan Evans.

A bridge marks the point of transition between formal pools that create a civic setting for the new extension and the more relaxed surroundings of the pond in the park. In the formal pool, a weir exploits a change in water level for visual and acoustic effect. The pond provides a freshwater habitat for a variety of pond life. A submerged safety margin

Kew Public Record Office

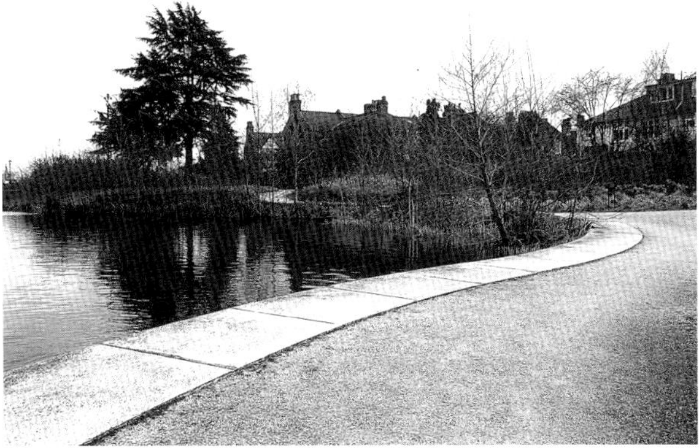

hillingdon to hammersmith & fulham

TBV Consult 1997

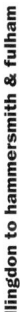

around most edges creates a permanent and stable 1.5-metre margin of shallow water. In spite of the delightful abundance of water in all its different forms, you are not aware of the closeness of the Thames. Surely this is a missed opportunity.

ADDRESS Ruskin Avenue, Kew, Surrey
CLIENT Public Record Office
RAIL Kew Gardens
ACCESS open Monday to Friday,
9.30–17.00

TBV Consult 1997

The Wetland Centre

The conversion of four redundant Victorian reservoirs and waterworks into 42.5 hectares of wetlands is no mean feat: 16 hectares of concrete-edged reservoirs broken up; more than 500,000 cubic metres of different soil types sorted and reused; more than 30 lakes, ponds and marshes built; 27 hydrological units; 600 metres of boardwalk; 27 bridges; 3.5 kilometres of pathway; seven hides; 27,000 new trees; more than 300,000 aquatic plants. The Wildfowl & Wetlands Trust claim it's the first wetland habitat to be created in any capital, on such a huge scale.

Public access is limited to paths that extend north and east of the visitor centre by architect John Thompson & Partners. On the east side visitors are encouraged to 'jet set around' 'Wetlands of the World'. 'Wetlands of the UK' is more interesting. Here the history of the reed-bed industry is celebrated and Land Art, Cleve West, Johnny Woodford, and Arne Maynard Garden Design have designed three 'sustainable gardens'. The intrepid visitor is rewarded at the end of each path by hides for 'twitching' and views of a somewhat surreal landscape. Views of Barrett homes compromise the effect but the project could not have been realised without them.

ADDRESS Queen Elizabeth's Walk, Barn Elms, London SW13
CLIENT Wildfowl & Wetland Trust
CONTRACT VALUE £16 million
TUBE Hammersmith, then short bus or taxi ride
TRAIN Barnes, short bus ride or 10-minute walk
ADMISSION adult £6.50; senior citizen £5.25; child £4.00
ACCESS open summer 9.30–18.00; winter 9.30–17.00 (closed Christmas day)

Wildfowl & Wetlands Trust/Adams Habermehl 2000

hillingdon to hammersmith & fulham

Wildfowl & Wetlands Trust/Adams Habermehl 2000

St Paul's Green

Hammersmith flyover is very much a part of London's urban fabric and is especially prominent in this particular landscape. The flat character of the land is accentuated by the horizontal lines and views that contrast strongly with the neighbouring high-rise office blocks.

It's now hard to imagine the area as a hostile environment, consisting of a series of purposeless green spaces sandwiched between St Paul's churchyard and the car park under the flyover – not a place to hang out on a dark winter's night. Whitelaw Turkington identified 'vitality' as the key to rejuvenation and sought to enliven the area by creating a route through the park, linking the Thames to Hammersmith Broadway via a tree-lined 'Broadwalk'. Existing crossing points over main roads connect with the route and form gateways to the park.

To encourage 'vitality', the park needed to feel like a safe place. Many of the trees were removed to ensure natural surveillance from nearby roads. Ground levels were also manipulated with safety in mind. The broad verge along Queen Caroline Street is built up behind a low 'sitting' wall. Widely spaced plane trees help to define the edge of the park and add a sense of enclosure without blocking views. A generous triangular lawn slopes away from the plane trees, lifting up at one corner. This in turn helps to model the space under the flyover.

The design does not seek to humanise the vast structure but rather to celebrate it with a colonnade of tall fastigiate hornbeams. The structure has also informed the language of materials: everything is big, bold, robust and functional, like the giant benches which are also used to direct cyclists. The designers saw the new Health Centre (by Guy Greenfield Architects) as an additional gateway and have used a similarly coloured concrete mix expressed in the building's pristine white walls for the cast-stone copings and pier caps. Underneath the flyover, the suggestion of an

Whitelaw Turkington 1998

Whitelaw Turkington 1998

St Paul's Green

activity centre (similar to the one under the Westway section of the A40) was dismissed by locals and ideas for lighting and water were rejected for cost reasons. Instead it has become another important pedestrian and cycle route to the Apollo and a mecca for skateboarders.

The area close to the grade II-listed church is more intimate and gardenesque. Most of the existing trees were removed (always a controversial move) to open up views to the church and expose a mature oak tree. Encircling low periwinkle and bulbs jostle for position against the remnants of gravestones. Cherry trees are planted in a more orderly fashion than their precedents to allow space for events and weddings.

Whitelaw Turkington consciously avoid creating 'finished' public open spaces, believing they should be allowed to evolve. The park relies on people to animate it – if you catch the park on an 'off-day' it can be uninspiring, but catch it at lunch time on a sunny day and you will find it full of life and packed with the local office community.

ADDRESS St Paul's Green, Hammersmith, London W6
CLIENT London Borough of Hammersmith and Fulham (section 106 agreement from Bredero Development)
SIZE 0.7 hectare
CONTRACT VALUE £600,000
TUBE Hammersmith
ACCESS open

Whitelaw Turkington 1998

hillingdon to hammersmith & fulham

Bechtel House Podium

Looking for somewhere peaceful and/or wacky to eat your sandwiches? Try this recently tarted-up secret roof garden. Raised above an existing car park, the short climb is guaranteed to leave you speechless rather than breathless. The only thing missing is some seating.

Part of the deal for L'Oreal's new headquarters by architects Marshall Cummings Marsh was to upgrade the multi-storey car-park roof. A temporary measure was required that would not compromise the crumbling structure of the concrete slab. The designers decided to introduce colour and create something attractive for the surrounding offices to look down on. Before and after comparisons can be made with the rest of the roof that's not owned by Standard Life.

Timber decking (crudely detailed) is floated over the existing roof creating a vast stage – Whitelaw Turkington boast that it's the largest timber deck in the UK. Eat your heart out Homefront team! Existing brick planters are rendered and painted pastel shades. The effect is truly cosmetic, I mean cosmic. The large galvanised-steel containers are an introduction. A long herbaceous border is planted along the north side with grasses and perennials. The garden will look at its best in spring when the multi-stem amelanchiers, underplanted with low-growing periwinkle, are in flower.

ADDRESS Hammersmith Road, London w6 – up steps to roof garden
CLIENT Standard Life
CONTRACT VALUE £470,000
TUBE Hammersmith
ACCESS open

Whitelaw Turkington 1999

Whitelaw Turkington 1999

kensington and chelsea

Emslie Horniman Pleasance Park

In 1913 Emslie Horniman (the local Liberal MP, 1906–10) observed that there was 'no place within a mile or so where children could play … nor anywhere for mothers and old people to rest' (quoted in *The Architects' Journal*, 28 January 1999). Inspired by Sister Ruth, renowned in the area for her charitable works, he bought an acre of open land off Kensal Road, presented it to the borough and 'dedicated it in perpetuity to the people of London as a recreation ground'. Horniman commissioned Charles Voysey to design his first and only park. It was expanded to 1.4 hectares after slum clearance in the 1960s.

The park is hemmed in by three distinctive landmarks: to the north the Grand Union Canal, to the south the Great Western Road, and to the east Ernö Goldfinger's Trellick Tower. Like many of our urban parks, it had fallen into disrepair and become a magnet for anti-social behaviour. Following riots in Notting Hill, the area was given priority attention by both local and central government. When North Kensington City Challenge came up with a proposal to rejuvenate it in 1996, the idea met with universal approval. Studio E Architects quickly realised that the City Challenge budget of £250,000 was not going to go far. They used it to apply for lottery funding and scored a triple whammy with a Heritage Lottery grant for the park, a Sports grant for a new sports pitch, and an Arts grant for the children's playground, gates, signage and fencing.

The Heritage Lottery grant restored the grade-II Voysey water garden (undertaken by Julian Harrap Architects) which in turn seems to have allowed a less conventional approach in the renovation of the wider park. Details such as pebbly paving, bespoke steel-edged timber benches, slender light sculptures, a wobbly steel fence and a Mediterranean palette of shrubs and perennials help create an environment that lifts it above a run-of-the-mill public park. An undulating rainbow-coloured landscape

Studio E/EDAW 1998

kensington and chelsea

shouts 'fun' from the new enclosed children's play area and seems to be extremely popular. The sports pitches have moved south, only to be replaced with yet another amphitheatre. The Quiet Garden is a new addition at the south-eastern corner of the park, with a sunken seating area, different types of stone sculpted into a variety of seats, and a bird bath. Its intended use could conflict with the adjacent pub. The central grass area has been enlarged by moving the existing play area west.

For three days in August the park becomes the launch pad for the Notting Hill Carnival. A chunk is taken out on the north side to create a wider pavement which looks a bit stark for the remaining 362 days of the year.

The first scheme to be completed with funding from the Heritage Lottery Fund's Urban Parks Programme, it has been hailed as a flagship inner-city regeneration project. Security is a major issue and the park has already suffered from vandalism, raising questions about the effectiveness of the consultation process. CCTV cameras mounted on tall masts can be seen as either comforting or inhibiting. In such a depressed area, perhaps it was wishful thinking to rely on self-policing. The borough is now stepping up police patrols and encouraging a community group, the Friends of Emslie Horniman Pleasance, to have more day-to-day involvement in security.

ADDRESS Kensal Road, London W10
CLIENT Royal Borough of Kensington and Chelsea
LEAD ARTIST Peter Fink
SERVICES ENGINEER Emanuel Smith
STRUCTURAL ENGINEER Adams Kara Taylor
CONTRACT VALUE £1.4 million
TUBE Ladbroke Grove/Westbourne Park
ACCESS open 7.30–dusk

Studio E/EDAW 1998

Emslie Horniman Pleasance Park

Kyoto Garden, Holland Park

Hana no kage Aka no tanin wa Nakari keri
[Beneath the cherry-blossom in the city park no one is lonely]
Issa, 1763–1827

Built as a souvenir of the Japanese Festival in 1991, the Kyoto Japanese garden is on the site of an earlier one, laid out by the Earl of Ilchester in the late nineteenth century when Holland Park was a private residence. The Kyoto garden is more authentic than you might think. It's a 'lake and stroll' garden as opposed to the 'dry-water' gardens more readily associated with Japan. Most Japanese gardens are based on styles and designs that originated from the Japanese Imperial Court at Kyoto. Japanese design traditions share some similarities with the eighteenth-century English Garden Landscape movement. Despite the garden's manicured appearance, asymmetry and contrasting textures represent a wilder version of nature. Blurred boundaries, raised levels and retained mature trees give the impression of a much larger garden.

The garden was raised in order to achieve a plateau and the first view of the garden is from the top of the steps. Visitors are encouraged to follow a bound gravel path – a trick to enable their experiences to be controlled. Every step is an opportunity to view a different angle and the sequence of Japanese artefacts is designed to evoke a series of nature scenes, sometimes fantastical. The cascade stones are arranged to accentuate the rate and drama of the water flow, contrasting with the horizontal lines of the bridge.

Materials were sourced in Britain (with the exception of the Japanese artefacts) including Scottish granite and 60 tons of Purbeck stone for the retaining wall – 220 tons of stone in total. Plant introductions from Japan in the nineteenth century to Britain's similarly temperate climate enabled

Kyoto Garden Association/HLM Landscape 1991

kensington and chelsea

Kyoto Garden Association/HLM Landscape 1991

Kyoto Garden, Holland Park

traditional plants such as pines, cherries, contorted willow, Japanese maples, azaleas, rhododendrons and prostrate juniper to be planted. Maintenance and management is vital, particularly as the plants are intended to be subordinate to the stones. The borough seems to be coping fairly well.

ADDRESS Holland Park, Kensington, London w8/w11
CLIENT Royal Borough of Kensington and Chelsea
WATER CONSULTANTS Water Techniques
SIZE 0.4 hectare
TUBE Holland Park
ACCESS open 7.30–dusk

Kyoto Garden Association/HLM Landscape 1991

Kyoto Garden Association/HLM Landscape 1991

Meanwhile Gardens

Sandwiched between the Grand Union Canal, Elkstone Road and Kensal Road lie Meanwhile Gardens. In the shadow of Trellick Tower, this type of neighbourhood park is a valuable asset, providing it can be made safe.

Regeneration of the linear park involved subdividing it into four areas and teasing out a distinct identity for each one. Beginning at the Great Western Road, the first area has a typical parkland character. Planet Earth reprofiled the ground levels, opened up views to the canal and provided a grass area for events. Paul McDermot helped remodel the concrete skate bowl, using a new material called Bendcrete. The play area for under-5s awaits a new building.

The gardens become increasingly wild as you go west, providing a stimulating environment for children and valuable cover for wildlife along the Grand Union Canal. The wildlife garden is essentially wooded, characterised by timber boardwalk introduced at intervals. The pond has been cleaned up and surrounded with dogwood, flag iris and other water-friendly species. A willow windbreak by Steve Pickup provides shelter from the high winds whipped up in the vicinity of Trellick Tower. There are plans for an office development in the most easterly garden, so it's been left as it is for the moment.

Integral to the design is a spiral path that links the areas together. It has a 'yellow brick road' quality, dressed with glittery stone (natural blue glass and Clearmac clear resin binder) with flared edges to allow people to pass (50mm x 50mm Baggeridge Brick clay cobbles). Entrances and exits are made more accessible to those with disabilities. Repetitive elements, such as oak railway sleepers for the leaning post and rail fencing and retaining walls, and the Corten steel lighting bollards and signs, help unite the scheme.

The scheme is informed by the wishes of the local community and the

Planet Earth 2000

designer was carefully selected by their representatives. The robust but unusual palette of materials bears the distinct trademark of Planet Earth. A few of the details appear to be rushed, like the timber, stone and gravel junction by the pond. It's a much less threatening environment than before, but it's vital that maintenance and management is kept up to scratch to sustain this.

ADDRESS Kensal Road and Elkstone Road, London W10
CLIENT Meanwhile Gardens Community Association (MGCA)
CONTRACT VALUE £500,000
SIZE 1.6 hectares
TUBE Westbourne Grove
ACCESS open

The Wildlife Garden, Natural History Museum

Tucked away at the west end of the South Kensington site and on the corner of the busy Cromwell Road and Queens Gate, it's no wonder the Natural History Museum's 'living gallery' is little known – it's the last place you would expect to find a wildlife garden. Gradually, the garden is gaining a reputation, especially thanks to four 'sheep in residence' invited to 'mow' the chalk downland meadow during summer 2000.

The garden was set up with three functions in mind: firstly to illustrate the potential for habitat creation and wildlife conservation in the inner city; secondly, to provide an educational resource to promote an understanding of the balance and relationship between plants and animals, for both child and adult visitors; and thirdly, to provide facilities for the life-sciences department of the museum to conduct ecological projects and to train staff in ecological monitoring work. The habitats are typical of lowland England: heathland (dry and wet), chalk downland, meadow, fen, three ponds, woodland areas to show different plant communities, hedgerows and an orchard. Some of these exist by virtue of excess elsewhere – turfs were imported from a disused quarry for the chalk downland meadow and peat was salvaged from ditch dredging for the fen.

Five years on, the garden is continuing to mature, evolve and change. Both the management and monitoring programmes are intensive. Six mature plane trees provide an unwelcome upper canopy layer, so trees beyond a certain height are coppiced, pollarded or transplanted to maintain structural diversity. Ornamental remnants from the previous formal gardens are slowly dying out. The hedgerows are ready for laying again and the battle against algae will continue to be waged in the ponds, despite the reed beds. A detailed fauna and flora survey carried out in 1997 and 1998 will be repeated in ten years. Meanwhile, a student from Imperial

The Adam Loxton Partnership/Natural History Museum 1995

The Wildlife Garden, Natural History Museum

The Adam Loxton Partnership/Natural History Museum 1995

kensington and chelsea

The Wildlife Garden, Natural History Museum

College monitors the effect of exhaust fumes on plants, a photographer records the early days of a nest of baby wrens, and a fox has been spotted. Only the frog spawn was deliberately introduced.

Lush vegetation and a labyrinthine path network make the garden exciting to explore, sometimes proving too irresistible to out-of-hours visitors. The beauty of an errant bindweed spiralling up a twig of field maple, thorny brambles bursting with unripe fruit and a rampaging wild clematis question the ethos that less is always more. Maybe there's hope that the English compulsive-obsessive disorder with neatly mown lawns can be cured.

ADDRESS Cromwell Road, London SW7
CLIENT Natural History Museum
ECOLOGISTS Dennis Vickers and Gary Grant, London Conservation Service
CONTRACT VALUE £200,000 (£50,000 from English Nature)
SIZE 0.4 hectare
TUBE South Kensington
ACCESS guided tours, May to September at 12.00, 3.00; open days, June to August, Tuesday, Thursday, Sunday, 13.00–16.00 (ask information desk for details on 020 7942 5725); also open as part of National Gardens Scheme

The Adam Loxton Partnership/Natural History Museum 1995

The Adam Loxton Partnership/Natural History Museum 1995

westminster

The Diana, Princess of Wales Memorial Playground

The fantasy world of Peter Pan has landed wholesale in the north-west corner of Kensington Gardens, complete with a giant pirate ship stranded on a sandy beach. Close by are rock pools, water jets, crocodile and mermaid rock. The character areas of beach cove and galleon, wigwam camp, treehouse encampment, tepee camp, movement and musical garden, mermaid's fountain and oak-tree village for under-3s are based on themes from J M Barrie's book. Barrie was a local resident and contributed towards the previous playground on this site laid out in 1909.

This is not your average playground. Due to its grade-1 parkland location, excavations below a 200mm depth were not permitted and natural materials and subdued colours were favoured. Recent European regulations on play equipment mean that it takes two years to get approval for new designs, so, despite its appearance, all the play equipment is off-the-peg from catalogues. Gravel and pebble paths swirl around from each of the areas, enclosed with live willow screens. An ambitious seaside planting scheme seems to be resisting the attacks of marauding youngsters, thanks to a continuous maintenance regime. Existing plane trees have been retained or transplanted and only three had to be removed.

The fact that the playground is continually heaving with children of all ages (0–12) and abilities is proof that the designers have succeeded in cracking many of the difficult issues connected with children's play. They claim to have balanced high play value with a certain amount of risk-taking. This is important as the playground is intended as a blueprint to encourage local authorities to follow suit. The criticism that the Peter Pan theme is out of touch with today's 'media-engrossed individual' (*RIBA Journal*, June 2000) is a sad reflection on our times and in reality that theme is only evident to the well-informed.

Land Use Consultants (LUC) 2000

The Diana, Princess of Wales Memorial Playground

westminster

Land Use Consultants (LUC) 2000

The Diana, Princess of Wales Memorial Playground

The playground is the government's (or rather the People's) memorial to Diana as opposed to a project financed by the Diana Memorial Fund. The latter has funded the refurbishment of Kensington Gardens and a £3 million walk laid out between the royal parks – Kensington Gardens, Hyde Park, Green Park and St James's Park – called The Diana, Princess of Wales Memorial Walk. The 11-kilometre-long circular route is charted by 80 plaques (sculpted by Alec Peever) set in the ground. Everything about the late Princess of Wales seems to arouse heated debate and it's easy to argue about whether or not these two tributes are fitting. Certainly they are much preferred to the memorial committee's initial proposal for a 32-acre 'modern-classical' memorial garden.

ADDRESS Kensington Gardens (north-west corner), London W2
CLIENT The Royal Parks Agency on behalf of the Diana, Princess of Wales Memorial Committee
SPECIALIST PLAY DESIGNER AND MANUFACTURER Richter Spielgerate (pirate ship and other play pieces)
ARTISTS John Buchanan, willow artist; Pater Appleton, sound posts; Reece Ingram, sheep sculptor; Totem Art, totem poles, Shelter Unlimited, tepees
CONTRACT VALUE £1.3 million
SIZE 0.7 hectare
TUBE Queensway
ACCESS open 10.00–19.30 (adults unaccompanied by children are not allowed to enter during playground hours. Between 9.30 and 10.00 during maintenance preparation period adults are allowed in)

Land Use Consultants (LUC) 2000

The Diana, Princess of Wales Memorial Playground

westminster

Land Use Consultants (LUC) 2000

The Great Courtyard, Somerset House

Cars have finally been kicked out of The Great Courtyard (formerly The Great Court) at Somerset House, reclaiming yet another important civic space for London. The scheme aims to create an appropriate setting for both Sir William Chambers' buildings and an art institution – a home for the Courtauld Collection – fit for the twenty-first century. The temptation to throw a glass roof over the space has been resisted.

Hand-sized granite setts were discovered during excavation work. The courtyard has been repaved with setts, similar in type, size and colour, visually uniting the building façades, laid in a simple pattern around those trendy fountains associated with Parc Citröen in Paris. The fountains rise up from the ground from metal plates that incorporate fibre-optic lights.

The courtyard is intended to be used for events and can hold up to 3500 people. Black metal uprights, to which barriers can be fixed, pop up from metal plates around the pavement edge. Electricity supplies to all sides of the square were first put to the test during the Covent Garden Festival in 2000, when a large screen relayed Haydn's *The Creation* from the Opera House.

The River Terrace is refurbished with a new café – cocktails a little pricey but worth it for the view. Most important of all, you can now walk from the South Bank over Waterloo Bridge, through Somerset House via the River Terrace to Covent Garden.

ADDRESS The Strand, London WC2
CLIENT Somerset House Trust
SIZE 4176 square metres
TUBE Embankment/Waterloo/Covent Garden
ACCESS open 8.00–23.00

Donald Insall Associates/Jeremy Dixon, Edward Jones 2000

The Great Courtyard, Somerset House

Donald Insall Associates/Jeremy Dixon, Edward Jones 2000

Hempel Square

To passers-by this may appear to be just another one of London's private garden squares. On closer inspection all is not as it seems. The private square now belongs to the second of Anouska Hempel's exclusive London hotels. The hotel is disguised as five Georgian mansions converted by Jestico + Whiles and the square is for the sole use of Hempel's guests. The best views are to be enjoyed from the privacy of the terrace or a bedroom balcony; lesser mortals can sneak a peek through the railings.

The square is an essay in studied elegance. Despite claims that it is inspired by the 'Zen spirit', the vocabulary appears to be essentially classical. Three square reflecting pools set within manicured lawns are laid out along a central axis and surrounded by white gravel paths, clipped box and yew hedging. The clean horizontal lines are punctuated at intervals with mop-head trees, Indian bean, magnolia, false acacia and topiary balls, box, privet and crenellated holly. Around the edge of the square the existing plane trees have been retained and under-planted with a dense layer of shade-loving shrubs and perennials.

London's garden squares are an important part of the city landscape. Now in its fourth year, London Garden Squares Day (organised by the London Historic Parks and Gardens Trust and English Heritage) allows the public to visit just a few of them. For more information, telephone 020 7839 3969 or 020 7973 3434.

ADDRESS Craven Hill Gardens, Craven Hill, London w2
CLIENT Fujita uk Ltd/Anouska Hempel
SIZE 0.3 hectare
TUBE Queensway
ACCESS open to hotel guests only

Anouska Hempel/Land Use Consultants 1994

Anouska Hempel/Land Use Consultants 1994

Serpentine Gallery

Originally private gardens for Queen Caroline, wife of George II, Kensington Gardens have retained their formal pattern of tree-lined walks set out in 1735 by landscape architect Charles Bridgeman. The gardens retain the feeling of large private grounds.

The gallery, formally a tea house, is situated at the convergence of two of Bridgeman's avenues. Its garden has recently been remodelled as part of a refurbishment programme funded by the Heritage Lottery fund. New horse chestnut trees are planted to restore the avenues, thereby creating a wedge-shaped garden at their apex. The main path off West Carriage Drive runs parallel to one of the avenues, mirrored by the park railings that enclose the garden. As a result the garden feels open and part of the wider parkland.

The design of the garden is consciously restrained, working both as a setting for the pavilion and as an open-air gallery. A series of slate benches carved by Ian Hamilton Finlay (his first permanent commission in London) is laid out in a sociable crescent shape facing Hyde Park. Yew hedges wrap around like crab pincers, with two catalpa trees planted as understudies to a pre-existing pair. A new stone circle (also by Finlay), inscribed with the Latin names of all the trees to be found in the park, marks the new entrance to the gallery from the south. Improved lighting makes it an attractive set-piece at night.

ADDRESS Kensington Gardens, London W2
CLIENT Serpentine Gallery Trust
CONTRACT VALUE £100,000 (excluding artwork)
TUBE South Kensington
ACCESS open daily, 10.00–18.00

Colvin and Moggridge 1997–98

Colvin and Moggridge 1997–98

Rose Garden, Hyde Park

The Rose Garden is whimsically laid out as a series of swirling beds and paths running parallel with Rotten Row, between the Serpentine and Hyde Park Corner. At the eastern end, the *Boy and Dolphin* fountain, displaced from Park Lane during road widening in 1960, now forms the centrepiece of the circular garden. Enclosed with yew hedging, and swags of climbing roses, it invites you to linger. The Diana fountain, out of scale and inaccessible in its old location, provides a focus for the next garden. The gardens are linked by a series of 'Agri-frame'-type pergolas smothered with climbing roses and interspersed with pleached lime trees.

This is not a rose garden in the traditional sense. The roses are mixed with a supporting cast of shrubs and perennials to provide interest throughout the year. Old-fashioned rose varieties gather round the Boy and Dolphin fountain, at a respectful distance from the louder modern varieties at the opposite end. The roses on display tend to have special characteristics such as repeat flowering, or are simply 'good doers'. They are fairly well labelled. It's the sort of garden that the punters love and designers love to hate, substantiating the truism that Britain is a nation of gardeners.

ADDRESS Hyde Park Corner, London SW1
CLIENT The Royal Parks Agency
CONTRACT VALUE £400,000
TUBE Hyde Park Corner
ACCESS open (subject to Hyde Park opening hours)

Colvin and Moggridge 1994–96

westminster

Colvin and Moggridge 1994–96

Stag Place Piazza

Anyone interested in public open spaces in London is bound to have heard of Stag Place. If you haven't seen it yet, hurry, as there are plans afoot to redevelop it. The project arose as part of a Section 106 planning gain agreement for Eland House and a competition held to improve this wind-swept and hostile 'space between buildings'. The winning design is a circle within a square – an architectural solution achieved by closing an adjacent road to traffic.

The circle is formed from curving sandstone walls creating a sheltered microclimate. The polished green lava stone coping provides an attractive contrast to the bright-red sandstone. There are colourful metal gates (closed at night) and a raised metal pergola. A green tinted glass building juts out into the piazza. Grassy banks rise to conceal plant rooms. There's a circular pool with a bubbling fountain and a curved bank of steps (yet another amphitheatre).

In the square outside, shrubberies of purple hazel, dogwood, laurustinus (*Viburnum tinus*), ornamental elder and euonymous lap against the walls. Trees are just beginning to poke their heads above the walls. An avenue of trees under-planted with blocks of yew hedging defines a pedestrian route. Bollards and expensive lighting columns are peppered about, but the budget appears to have dried up where the paving is concerned. Cheap paving bricks and concrete setts stand out against the high specification of everything else.

The corporate character of the space gives off confusing signals – it's not clear whether the public are really welcome here. Surrounded by tall buildings, the piazza is almost permanently in shade. Its imminent disposal due to a development proposal and the fact that the café building has never had a tenant speak volumes. This is a clear lesson in the importance of understanding the wide range of factors that need to be consid-

Renton Howard Wood Levin Partnership 1997

Stag Place Piazza

Renton Howard Wood Levin Partnership 1997

Stag Place Piazza

ered when creating a new public space.

A 20-metre-high giant screen of coloured blobs designed by Patrick Heron and Feary and Heron Architects provides a windbreak and gateway to the piazza. At first glance it is tempting to associate it with the nearby Mövenpick hotel. The more perceptive might just make out a map of Stag Place.

ADDRESS Stag Place, London SW1
CLIENTS Land Securities and Westminster Council
STRUCTURAL/WIND ENGINEER Ove Arup & Partners
SERVICES ENGINEER Roger Preston & Partners
CONTRACT VALUE £3 million
TUBE Victoria
ACCESS open, closes at dusk

Renton Howard Wood Levin Partnership 1997

Renton Howard Wood Levin Partnership 1997

Queen Victoria Memorial

The recent pedestrianisation of the space outside Buckingham Palace has converted a dangerous traffic roundabout into an important civic space. The scheme gives long-overdue priority to pedestrians, respects the setting, and could be considered a forerunner to the future World Squares initiative. It received a commendation in the 1996 Civic Trust Awards.

Radical in terms of logistics, the treatment is low-key and easily taken for granted. However, it involved rerouting traffic to create a car-free zone between the memorial and the palace. The piazza is a sea of red tarmac, reading as a continuous surface with the Mall and Constitution Hill, part of the ceremonial (red carpet?) route to Kensington Palace. Cast-iron bollards set in granite setts are relied on to define the car-free zone. Over such an expansive area the plethora of posts can be confusing.

Architect Terry Farrell has claimed that the original idea to improve the public areas around Buckingham Palace is his. More recently he has argued that they're being implemented to the 'design of the municipal traffic engineer rather than with the kind of style, vision and sense of scale … that a Continental city would have' (*Building Design*, 19 November 1999). Inspired by the crowds that thronged The Mall and royal parks after the death of Diana, Princess of Wales, his grand vision is to create a continuous belt of greenery stretching 4 km from Trafalgar Square in the east to Kensington in the west. This is to be achieved by pulling down the walls and fences around Buckingham, St James's and Kensington Palaces. Naturally, not every Londoner is taken with this idea.

ADDRESS Buckingham Palace, London SW1
CLIENT The Royal Parks Agency
TUBE St James's Park/Green Park
ACCESS open

Land Use Consultants 1995

Queen Victoria Memorial

Land Use Consultants 1995

St James's Park Playground

The playground, with swings, slides, a see-saw and little Wendy house modelled on the lake boat house, is tucked away towards the south-west corner of the park. It's been pushed further towards the lake than its tatty predecessor, which used to spoil the view. This involved realigning an existing path.

It's not just another fenced enclosure with play equipment. The retention of existing trees, use of natural materials, manipulation of levels and position of shrub beds allow the playground to blend into its surroundings so successfully that it's easy to miss.

Large boulders, porphyry and granite setts edge a series of sandpits, bridged in one place by a particularly large stone. Paths and steps lead off to a series of separate compartments carved out on different levels, to fit snugly around the boles of several majestic plane trees.

The scheme is not only sympathetic to its surroundings but offers far more opportunities for creative play than your average flat-as-a-pancake playground.

ADDRESS St James's Park, London SW1
CLIENT The Royal Parks Agency
ENGINEER C J Witham & Partners
CONTRACT VALUE £240,000
TUBE Victoria/St James's Park
ACCESS open during park opening hours; no unaccompanied adults

Colvin and Moggridge 1994

Colvin and Moggridge 1994

Horse Guards Parade

Horse Guards Parade is imprinted in most British minds as the home of the annual Trooping of the Colour ceremony. The parade ground is contained on three sides by an assortment of buildings symbolising the imperial past of the nation. William Kent's grade 1-listed buildings (1740s) occupy the central position looking west to London's most renowned landscape garden. St James's Park is famous for its views outwards, and the view looking back from the bridge towards Whitehall Court and Horse Guards is arguably the most important.

Until recently it was a car park for the remaining 364 days of the year. Its relationship with the park was jeopardised by Horse Guards Road and it had become a very inward-looking space.

By removing the traffic, Horse Guards Parade can now be better appreciated by the estimated 15 million people who visit St James's Park every year. Colvin and Moggridge claim the scheme is deliberately minimalist to 'allow the elegance and dignity of the surrounding buildings to dominate'. Two of the trees (planted 40–50 years ago) that align the road were cut down to open up the historic view towards the lake. A continuous gravel surface now links the parade ground to the park, which is not as simple as it might sound. It involved a battle to retain the nostalgic crunch of loose gravel and extensive research into the anti-skid properties of various types of gravel. The final decision was to use 6mm Chinese bauxite gravel and this was one of first instances where epoxy resin has been used to bind the surface.

But the scheme is only half complete. Horse Guards is still an inward-looking space, thanks to continued vehicular presence on the road and the position of the Guards Memorial. Hope may be at hand with the future World Squares initiative. Foster & Partners' proposals to pedestrianise Trafalgar and Parliament Squares include the closure of Horse

Colvin and Moggridge 1997

Horse Guards Parade

Colvin and Moggridge 1997

Horse Guards Parade

Guards Road to form a safe, traffic-free link – with the exception of cycles, essential access and VIPs – between the two squares. This would achieve full reunification of the park and parade ground and help to strengthen the route to the river along Horse Guards Avenue.

ADDRESS St James's Park, London SW1
CLIENT The Royal Parks Agency
CONSULTANT ENGINEER Peter Brett Associates
CONTRACT VALUE £1.1 million
TUBE Charing Cross/Westminster
ACCESS open

Colvin and Moggridge 1997

Colvin and Moggridge 1997

Tate Britain Centenary Development

Tate Britain is determined not to be upstaged by its attention-seeking, crowd-pulling sibling across the water. In celebration of its centenary it's being treated to a new entrance off Atterbury Street by John Miller & Partners and a spanking new garden. No expense is being spared.

The garden is an exercise in restraint; it refuses to compete with the architecture. A bold geometric layout relates to the building's symmetry and significant axis. The language of materials – natural stone, grass, yew hedging – is distinctly classical but a contemporary interpretation allows geometrical planes to float over one another. Elements such as a stainless-steel edge to retain the lawn squares introduce a modern feel.

The main single element is a vast 'mat' of Portland stone that unifies the disparate external spaces. The stone is peeled back, cut out, and scuffed up in strategic places. The concept is best understood by looking at the work around the Clore Gallery. Here the new layout both respects and incorporates an earlier layer. The sunken water garden is refurbished with new water lilies and new York stone (Crossland Hills) steps inserted.

Following a great garden-design tradition, the garden is broken down into a series of rooms. Seasonal plants will change the character of the minimalist herbaceous borders at different times of the year. The south garden is complete; the west entrance is scheduled for completion in 2001.

ADDRESS Millbank, London SW1
CLIENT Trustees of the Tate Britain
HORTICULTURAL CONSULTANT Schoenaich Rees Landscape Architects
SIZE 5757 square metres
TUBE Pimlico
ACCESS open 10.00–17.50; closed 24, 25, 26 December

Allies and Morrison 2000–

Allies and Morrison 2000–

National Gallery Sainsbury Wing

This small urban piazza is slotted between the National Gallery and Robert Venturi's Sainsbury Wing extension. It acts as a gateway for the Jubilee Walk that links Leicester Square and Trafalgar Square. The scheme resembles Venturi's original concept design. Cube-shaped plane trees are laid out on a grid, their grilles surrounded by York stone and granite. The trees are illuminated at night by up-lighters.

It's hard to believe such a small site could be so controversial. The borough was opposed to the idea of plane trees, arguing that they are prone to disease and not an appropriate street tree. Even the decision to use natural stone was a battle, due to the gallery's fast-evaporating budget. Thankfully, wisdom prevailed but the proposed seating has lost out.

The London plane (*Platanus x hispanicus*) was introduced in the 1680s from Portugal. It is now Britain's largest broad-leaved hardwood and unlike many other trees can tolerate high levels of pollution. It is known to suffer from occasional fungal decay and can be distressed by cable laying and salt spread on roads in winter. The oldest are thought to grow in Berkeley Square, but as yet no one knows how long they live. If they all start to die at the same time, the character of the London landscape will change dramatically. Plans are afoot to begin a slow replacement planting programme.

ADDRESS Trafalgar Square, London SW1
CLIENT National Gallery
CONTRACT VALUE £30,000 approximately (soft landscape)
SIZE 300 square metres
TUBE Charing Cross/Leicester Square
ACCESS open

Armstrong Bell Landscape Design 1992

westminster

Armstrong Bell Landscape Design 1992

Leicester Square

Still claiming to be one of London's largest pedestrianised zones (it's hard to believe it's larger than Covent Garden), this scheme represents an important milestone for the now almost non-existent in-house local-authority design teams.

By the mid 1980s, Leicester Square had become a dark and threatening crime-ridden place, highlighted by vacant premises on all the approach roads. Previous attempts by the GLC had involved partial pedestrianisation of two sections of the square, but people ignored the bollards and continued to park there. In the eighteenth century it was laid out as a cruciform, a layout that had continued in varying forms but one that no longer responded to people movement in the modern era. Local residents and businesses pressurised the council to take action.

Any refurbishment was destined to be controversial – Westminster had their reputation for thorough consultation to uphold. Four years of consultation, five scheme options and a court case later (Leicester Square is still one of the leading cases in Covenant Law), it's amazing anything happened at all. During this drawn-out process, Westminster had the foresight and confidence to appeal for private sponsorship. London Electricity Board (LEB) took the bait and offered a major financial contribution in exchange for the underground soil rights. The schemes by five external consultants were finally thrown out (having helped crystallise the issues) and the in-house team was given the green light to crack on with their 'garden option'.

The most ground-breaking aspect of the scheme is the pedestrianisation of not only the square but also eight associated streets. Access is restricted by electronically controlled barriers at the end of the streets. The square itself is treated like a traditional London square, with a railed garden at the centre of a simple paved area. Clutter is restricted – street

Westminster City Council 1992

Westminster City Council 1992

3.32

lights are confined to the building façades; the number of litter bins has been reduced; and shrub planting is concentrated at focal points and gateways. Expensive pink granite flags – costing four times the amount Westminster would normally spend – are laid in the square, with York flagstones, instead of concrete paviors, for the side streets.

The scheme deals with old problems as opposed to creating new attractions – a case of taking out rather than putting in – though the flag poles, Silver Jubilee Walk plaques, Commonwealth mileage indicators and theatreland kiosk by architects APT Partnership, which partially disguises the LEB substation, are new. On-site management of security barriers, video cameras, and bird-scarers is provided for. Shakespeare's memorial and other historic busts are still there to discover, and the square continues to suffer from an overdose of bollards.

The jury is still out. Norman Foster once described it as '... one of Europe's most exciting and civilised public spaces ...'; Richard Rogers is not of the same opinion. Whatever your opinion may be, Leicester Square's popularity with tourists is beyond argument.

ADDRESS Leicester Square, London WC2
CLIENT Westminster City Council
ENGINEERING PROJECT MANAGEMENT Howard, Humphreys, Brown & Root (phase 1)
CONTRACT VALUE £4 million (including £2.4 million from LEB)
SIZE 12,500 square metres
TUBE Leicester Square
ACCESS open (gardens close at dusk)

westminster

Westminster City Council 1992

westminster

RIBA Roof Terrace

This is a story of designer triumph over institutional adversity. Fraught with controversy, the terrace had become an uninviting place, providing storage for Patisserie Valerie and occasional exhibition space. So how did two freshly qualified garden designers succeed where members of the establishment had failed before? Elsie Josland and Helen McCabe dreamt up their idea following regular visits to the café and bookshop. Undeterred by the RIBA's lack of funds, they found sponsors. Allies and Morrison were assigned to monitor their works.

Mobile marine-ply planters covered with a galvanised skin now occupy positions on two sides of the terrace. Yew and box hedges provide an evergreen foil for perennials. The yew are ultimately intended to interrupt the horizontal line of the wall coping. Two mobile planters planted with Himalayan birch trees (*Betula jacquemontii*) allow the terrace to continue as an exhibition space. A brilliant-white Spar gravel mulch sets off the planting and a coia-based compost was concocted to keep the weight down, with lica (a free-draining material) at the base of each planter. The scheme incorporates a pre-existing William Pye sculpture-fountain. Unfortunately, funding did not stretch to the drab paving slabs.

ADDRESS Royal Institute of British Architects (RIBA), 66 Portland Place, London W1
CLIENT Royal Institute of British Architects
SPONSORS British Steel, Patisserie Valerie, Clifton Nurseries, Roffrey Ltd, H2O
CONTRACT VALUE £15,000
SIZE 150 square metres
TUBE Great Portland Street/Oxford Circus
ACCESS open, subject to RIBA opening hours (telephone 020 7580 5533)

McCabe Josland 1998

westminster

McCabe Josland 1998

city of london

1 Fleet Place

1 Fleet Place is part of an office development strip by Skidmore, Owings & Merrill stretching between Holborn Viaduct and Ludgate Circus. Like Broadgate (see page 4.16) – but with less spatial scope – it's as much about new squares and pedestrian routes as buildings, providing facilities for office workers and the public and making a marketing statement to attract investors. The smaller spaces continue a tradition that's more in keeping with the fabric of the old City.

The scheme is similar to Broadgate's Exchange Square (with the same design team). Complex engineering solutions have been found to build over railway tracks. This involved rerouting a main railway line, removing a viaduct (including a rail bridge that had obscured a view to St Paul's since Victorian times) and constructing a new subsurface station.

The main piazza is at the entrance to 1 Fleet Place with L-shaped sections of yew hedging and false acacia trees (*Robina pseudoacacia* 'Bessoniana'). These create an interesting entrance, a series of inward-looking compartments that can function as outdoor offices, and enclosed seating for a café. The layout respects a natural diagonal desire line from New Fleet Lane to City Thameslink.

The language of hard materials is also similar to Exchange Square. Look out for the jet-black polished granite wall, large galvanised containers and seating alcoves carved out of the side of the building and planted overhead with heathers and ivy.

ADDRESS 1 Fleet Place, London EC4
CLIENT Rosehaugh Stanhope
TUBE Blackfriars
RAIL City Thameslink
ACCESS open

Hanna/Olin/Charles Funke Associates 1993

Hanna/Olin/Charles Funke Associates 1993

Petershill Steps

The Petershill development lies to the south of St Paul's cathedral, contained by Carter Lane to the north and Queen Victoria Street to the south. A new scheme by Rolfe Judd Architects to replace a 1960s office complex provided an opportunity to improve the existing view and approach to St Paul's from the Thames, and also to enhance the setting of the College of Arms and St Nicholas Cole Abbey. This all involved close liaison with English Heritage, the Royal Fine Art Commission, the College of Arms and the Dean and Chapter of St Paul's.

Until recently, two awkward flights of steps obscured and compromised views of the south-facing portico. The replacement small flights of steps and long landings have created a processional approach with continuous views of Wren's masterpiece. A series of 1:20 ramps (the steepest gradient permitted without hand rails) cuts diagonally across the steps, attracting skateboarders like bees to a honeypot. Nothing is allowed to obscure or conflict with the view, from the intentionally dull offices to the line of tall gingko trees (*Gingko biloba*) set well back.

To the east of the steps a series of connected piazzas and courtyards and a café-cum-restaurant deal effortlessly with the steep changes in levels. Disabled access is via a lift in the restaurant. Opening up Distaff Lane restored the view to the guild church of St Nicholas Cole Abbey.

A limited palette of natural stone materials creates a corporate identity for the development. Main areas are paved with York stone, and the steps are in flame-textured granite. Cobbles are reintroduced to the streets and Portland stone is laid in the vicinity of the guild church. Square stone bollards double as seats; rogue bollards proudly bearing the arms of the Corporation of London appear amusingly out of context. In addition to the gingkos, honey locust trees (*Gleditsia triacanthos*) are planted in shady enclaves, with pin oaks (*Quercus palustris*), selected for their

Charles Funke Associates 1997

city of london

4.6

matching formal shapes) and London plane trees.

Petershill Steps have jumped unexpectedly into the limelight with the new Millennium Bridge to Tate Modern. Plans for a bridge between St Paul's and Bankside date back to before the First World War, but it's a 'happy accident' (according to *Building Design*, 31 March 2000) that the bridge lines up with the new steps.

ADDRESS Peters Hill, London EC4
CLIENT MEPC Developments Ltd
CONTRACT VALUE £1.8 million
TUBE St Paul's
ACCESS open

Charles Funke Associates 1997

city of london

25 Cannon Street

On the site of an existing public space, the new garden is reorientated to provide an attractive setting and entrance to Fidelity Investments' new office block designed by Renton Howard Wood Levin Partnership (RHWL). St Paul's provides an impressive backdrop.

The garden is pushed away from the building by a generous band of Purbeck stone and enclosed on three sides by a low sitting wall. Conceived as a London garden square, the centrepiece is a gently concave oval lawn. The path circuit widens in places to allow space for shortcuts to Blackfriars. The lawn is stepped up to discourage people cutting across it, but it's been laid as a golf green (i.e. on an 80 per cent sand bed) just in case.

Wide shrubberies, jam-packed with trees and shrubs provide privacy and block out views of passing traffic. Every detail has been chewed over. There are large planes and Raywood ash (*Fraxinus angustifolia* 'Raywood') trees and an unusual collection of ornamental shrubs, including dogwoods, Japanese maples, Judus trees (*Cercis siliquastrum*) and a parrotia (*Parrotia persica*). Each border is planted according to its aspect.

From his new plinth, the bust of Admiral Philips (salvaged from the previous building) surveys the scene. The juxtaposition of the informal planting and the formal elevation seems to work well. The greatest challenge is whether the public will respect and look after it.

ADDRESS 25 Cannon Street, London EC4
CLIENT Fidelity Investments
CONTRACT VALUE £650,000
TUBE St Paul's
ACCESS open

Elizabeth Banks Associates 2000

Elizabeth Banks Associates 2000

Roof Garden, No. 1 Poultry

The roof garden lies on top of one of London's most controversial buildings, described as 'London's post-modern flagship' (S Hardingham, *London: a guide to recent architecture*, 1999). It's one of the few roof gardens within the square mile and one of the first commercial roof gardens to be created in London since Derry and Toms' famous garden on the roof of the old department store in Kensington High Street.

Lord Palumbo approached Arabella Lennox-Boyd back in 1985, asking her to work with James Stirling to design a roof garden that would provide 'an oasis in the City, where office roof-tops are usually covered in mechanical plant, not botanical ones'. Planning permission was finally given in 1988, but work on the garden didn't begin until 1995. Following the death of James Stirling, Lennox-Boyd and her team worked with Michael Wilford and Partners.

Access is via a glass elevator that brings you out opposite the entrance to Terence Conran's Coq d'Argent restaurant. The garden provides seating for up to 100 diners. There are great views down the open circular core with its brilliant-blue-glazed tiles to the courtyard below.

The triangular layout is divided into three areas: an inner garden, an apex garden and two side gardens. The inner garden acts as an 'oasis' surrounding the central core. A colossal oak pergola walkway around the perimeter allows waiters to circulate at speed. White wisteria and edible grapes (*Uva fragola*) are beginning to smother it, framing charming views across the courtyard. Tables and chairs nestle against the lush foliage that contrasts with the formality of the triangular grey granite paving slabs. Mediterranean shrubs such as lavender, rosemary, iris, acanthus and Cistus are more tolerant of the extreme conditions than the roses, camelias and jasmine. The shrub beds are raised to allow a soil depth of 750mm in places (over a reservoir board and roof barriers by Euroroof). Sixteen

Arabella Lennox-Boyd 1998

Arabella Lennox-Boyd 1998

mature fruit-bearing trees, including cherry, crab apple, magnolia and hawthorn, reflect the garden's culinary associations and are secured to the roof with an underground guy system.

A set of bronze gates opens on to the apex garden and a spectacular panorama of the city. The lawn falls away from your feet, contained by protective rails at the edges. The clever change in levels allows you to see but not touch the apex garden. Lennox-Boyd claims the stripes of clipped box are inspired by ploughed fields. Stone spheres, chosen in preference to topiary to keep the weight down and lit from beneath, appear to float at night.

Views from the restaurant to the two side gardens are less impressive. Arms of columnar beech hedging echo the pergola, underplanted with white roses and Cotoneaster species.

ADDRESS 1 Poultry, London EC2
CLIENTS Trizec Hahn/Palumbo Partnership
STRUCTURAL ENGINEER Ove Arup & Partners
SIZE 0.2 hectare
TUBE Bank (take exit 9)
ACCESS limited, accessible to diners at Le Coq d'Argent

Arabella Lennox-Boyd 1998

Roof Garden, No. 1 Poultry

city of london

Arabella Lennox-Boyd 1998

Monkwell Square

The overall design principles are sound, if expensive. But like Farrell's architecture, Monkwell Square will probably not equate with most people's idea of 'taste'.

Approach Monkwell Square from Bastion Highwalk and it's hard to miss. Part of the Alban Gate development that projects over London Wall, the square and new housing stands out as a neo-classical set piece. A fortified garden rises from the centre of the square like a colour-co-ordinated meringue complete with cherry, or rather stone obelisk, on top, elevated on a plinth of brick and stone. Cars parked in bays around its base disappear into the background.

The garden is designed to be viewed from above, rather than being a place to sit and read a book in. Six lollipop trees encircled by yew hedges rise out of the bastions that form the four corners, underplanted with variegated ivy. Large yew topiary on either side of a central path leads to a little belvedere. The evergreens of the trees and shrubs complement the bright red and white stone- and brickwork.

ADDRESS Monkwell Square, London EC2
CLIENT MEPC Developments Ltd
TUBE Barbican
ACCESS open

Terry Farrell and Partners 1992

Monkwell Square

Terry Farrell and Partners 1992

Broadgate

Broadgate is 'widely considered to be the best office complex in Europe' (*Building Design*, 22 October, 1999). The development, another brain-child of Stuart Lipton, stretches from Finsbury Avenue to Liverpool Street Station and as far north as Bishopsgate. Cars are banished underground in a space the height of a pantechnicon, creating the opportunity for a network of 'greened' public spaces at ground level. It was masterplanned by Arup Associates and built in two phases.

Begin at Finsbury Avenue Square and work east to Phase 2. Here the dark, reflective quality of Arup's buildings gives the square a sombre char-acter. In spring they are lit up by the shoots of the new leaves of the sugar maples (*Acer saccharinum*), underplanted with lonicera (*Lonicera pileata*), cherry laurel (*Prunus laurocerasus*, 'zabeliana') and ivy.

Broadgate Square is dominated by a circular arena ('the most successful public space in London', according to Space Syntax research) that converts into an ice-skating rink in winter. The outer edges of the circle rise up in densely greened terraces. Russian vine and wisteria planted to make a quick impact were removed once ivy was established. Shrubs planted to create the green cascade include mahonia (*M. japonica*), trumpet vine (*Campsis radicans*), viburnum (*V. rhytido-phyllum* and *V. opulus*) and cotoneaster (*C. x suecicus* 'Skogholm'). A row of pleached silver limes (*Tilia tormentosa*) is a reminder of the more traditional method of creating green cabinets. Cafés on the middle terraces provide vantage points to people-watch at lunchtime.

To the north, Sun Street roundabout forms a 'green gateway' to Broad-gate, planted with a ring of hornbeam and under-planted with ivy. It's well maintained and proof that a good-looking scheme is a healthy one.

Phase 2 areas (designed by Skidmore, Owings & Merrill, Inc. and Hanna/Olin) lie to the north and east. With better-quality stone, they

Arup Associates/Hanna/Olin/Charles Funke Associates 1984–

Arup Associates/Hanna/Olin/Charles Funke Associates 1984–

appear more solid – in fact they could not be less so for Exchange Square is suspended over Liverpool Street's railway tracks. Take a look at the inside of the vaulted train sheds if you don't believe me. This is no ordinary roof garden – there are factors such as 24-hour air movement to consider. A curved red sandstone wall encloses the end of an expansive piece of lawn (a first for Broadgate – apparently croquet is played on it!), with a raised granite edge providing informal seating. An avenue of 22 horse chestnut trees is elevated on a stone platform. This allows the rootballs to be suspended in a linear trench (65 metres long and 2 metres deep) which provides them with a continuous root run. The trees emerge directly from removable pre-cast concrete covers, which look rather odd.

The bold mass plantings give a sense of continuity to the disparate mix of architectural surfaces and public artworks. In this highly artificial and high maintenance environment, Charles Funke Associates have tried to ensure the best planting conditions possible. But despite an intensive maintenance regime Broadgate is beginning to look dated and tired. British Land recognises it is due for a facelift. Promises of further enhancements include 'new landscaping' in the Arena, Finsbury Avenue Square and Sun Street and 'new stone finishes' to Broadgate Arena, improved pedestrian access and new signs and lighting.

ADDRESS Broadgate, London EC2
CLIENT Rosehaugh Stanhope Development plc in conjunction with British Rail Property Management Board (since 1994 Broadgate has been owned by British Land Company)
SIZE 3.6 hectares
TUBE Liverpool Street
ACCESS open

Arup Associates/Hanna/Olin/Charles Funke Associates 1984–

Arup Associates/Hanna/Olin/Charles Funke Associates 1984–

Lloyds Register of Shipping

The old churchyard of St Katherine Coleman, hidden behind the magnificent façade of the Lloyds shipping building, is now moonlighting as the entrance forecourt to the latest Lloyds building by Richard Rogers Partnership. Most of its guts are ripped out, but the new scheme elegantly combines remnants of the old with new elements.

The canopies of two mature trees – London plane and Tree of Heaven (*Ailanthus altissima*) – provide an instant roof, enlivening the space in sunlight with dancing, dappled shadows. They also break up the impact of the seemingly endless metal shafts (the new offices) that soar above, which would otherwise overwhelm such a small space. Raised shrub beds are edged with generous granite copings and informally positioned timber seats. The spiky phormiums and irises are regimented in rows to contrast with cushions of evergreen groundcover, a recurrent theme in Hutchison's schemes.

The abstract floor layout is best appreciated from the external glass lifts. A bound gravel surface brings cohesion to a widely spread group of tight spaces, both inside and outside the building. Textural detail is picked out in granite and York stone. The raised pool and fountain lend the charm of a modern-day oasis.

ADDRESS Fenchurch Street, London EC3
CLIENT Lloyds Register of Shipping
CONTRACT VALUE £180,000
TUBE Tower Hill
RAIL Fenchurch Street
ACCESS open

Edward Hutchison Landscape Architects 1999

Edward Hutchison Landscape Architects 1999

islington and hackney

Edward Square

'Edward Square is fantastic' is the only graffiti this neighbourhood park has suffered, according to the designer, Johanna Gibbons. A testimony to rigorous consultation that not only secured Single Regeneration Budget (SRB) funding but is crucial for the park's survival in this inner-city area that includes the Barnsbury Conservation Area and the Bemerton estate.

During the 1960s the square was cleared of all housing, having been badly bombed in the Second World War. By the 1980s, following a long campaign to classify it as open space, it had become a flat, featureless site. The possibility of SRB funding in the 1990s provided the catalyst for a group of local campaigners to take action. They appointed Gibbons to consult the community and to prepare a design and bid.

Two months of consultation work culminated in a Planning for Real exercise. One hundred people were enticed there, with free raffle tickets for those who registered their details. Gibbons visited youth clubs to appeal to 13- to 21-year-olds, likely to be the most destructive group. The park was planned as a place for old and young, with trees and flowers, a kick-about area, with access for cyclists and roller-bladers but no dogs.

The main entrance leads to a small orchard with a native flowering meadow, the only area where dogs are allowed. A cobbled path (Mount Sorrel granite) keeps its uneven state as a reminder of the square's history. Turf-jointed paving slabs have been plug-planted with rosemary, thyme, lavender and sage (an attractive example of sustainable urban drainage). The weeping willow tree is a replacement for an existing one that had to be felled – a film recorded the process, and local children made sculptures from willow whips. Fixed chairs are arranged in sociable circles under several different types of ornamental crab-apples. A pair of galvanised entry gates announces the entrance to the main park, decorated with brightly coloured designs by local youngsters.

J & L Gibbons 2000

Edward Square

islington and hackney

Edward Square

The park is divided into four main areas including two large lawns, either side of an area paved with granite aggregate slabs where play equipment and seating are laid out. One lawn is for picnicking, with honey locust trees (*Gleditsia triacanthos* 'Inermis') standing in long grass and 21,500 bulbs planted by local children. The other is a more closely mown area for kicking a ball about and festivals. It is enclosed on two sides by a long stepped seat that's been shot-blasted (by Gary Breeze) with the words of a poem by Andrew Motion. A line of oriental Plane trees (*Platanus x acerifolia*) filters views to the nearby school. A nature area planted with native trees and shrubs provides an educational resource.

A decorative wall panel (by artist Kate Blee) brightens up a long wall, painted with pure mineral colours in a rectilinear pattern. A white line at the height of a tennis net should stimulate creative ball games. Brick foundations discovered during excavation work are recycled as seats, along the alignment of the back wall of the old terrace.

The community has been involved at every stage of the process. A group of children even interviewed the contractor and monitored the work on site. Between 300 and 400 people turned up to a Millennium party, a sign that the whole process was worth it.

ADDRESS Copenhagen Street/Caledonian Road, London N1
CLIENTS Edward Square Steering Group and London Borough of Islington on behalf of funders King's Cross Partnership
CONTRACT VALUE £310,000
SIZE 0.49 hectare
TUBE King's Cross
RAIL Caledonian Road /Barnsbury
ACCESS open

J & L Gibbons 2000

J & L Gibbons 2000

Owen's Fields

This pocket-park doesn't blow the senses, but it is illustrative of a general trend. Due to planning pressure and prevailing common sense, some developers are beginning to see the advantage of improving the environment of a place *before* developing it.

The design is characteristic of Whitelaw Turkington's unfussy approach to public spaces. Several mature plane trees along one boundary help to give the park an instant sense of enclosure in the absence of buildings. The sinuous shape of a broadly curving gravel path running through the park is said to be inspired by the ancient course of the New River beneath this part of Islington. A bespoke timber bench defines the inside edge of the path and also the perimeter of a circular lawn. Opposite, clumps of multi-stem birch trees and single-stem pears are grouped to form alcoves. A mixture of shade-tolerant evergreen shrubs surround the edges of the park, including Mexican orange blossom (*Choisya ternata*) and pyracantha species, and shrubby perennials such as Christmas roses and sage.

New River Walk is a short walk away (off Canonbury Road) but well worth a visit. It's a series of linear gardens created for the public by Islington Council (1953–54) along the route of the seventeenth-century New River aqueduct. Restoration started in 1996 and is almost complete.

ADDRESS Owen Street, London EC1
CLIENT The Worshipful Company of Brewers
CONTRACT VALUE £100,000
SIZE 0.25 hectare
TUBE Angel
ACCESS open

Whitelaw Turkington 1996

Whitelaw Turkington 1996

Hackney Community College

This multiple-award-winning scheme is the largest further-education development in the country (*Landscape Design*, May 1999). Two expansive courtyards lie at the heart of the complex, a layout much favoured by Hampshire County Architects. New-build and existing Edwardian buildings enclose this 'haven of learning', creating a comfortable microclimate. The courtyards are subdivided into a hierarchy of undefined subspaces, to serve the wide ranging needs of the multicultural mix of mature students. Originally members of the community were to be allowed to use the place, but due to security concerns a swipe-card system now operates and only students are allowed in. Public art is a major element of the design, securing vital funding.

The two courtyards differ in character. The north courtyard is predominantly hard; a geometrical layout with large areas of paving is designed to cope with the volume of students. Elevated areas of grass take on a more ornamental status, like modern-day Oxford quadrangles. Artistic seating includes a stone bench by Bettina Fumee, carved with the poem, *A State of Rock*, by Benjamin Zephaniah, and *Quarry* seat sculptures (by Pat Kaufman). The public library and learning resource centre occupy a central position at lower ground-floor level, overlooking a stone amphitheatre and sunken water garden and *Blue Wall* by Susannah Heron, (currently waiting to be repaired). Retained existing trees make strong vertical statements, breaking up the building mass and providing instant harmony between old and new.

The south courtyard layout is also geometrical, but softer and more low key. As a result the less-intimidating lawns are well worn. Shrub borders block-planted with hebes, laurustinus, broom, cotoneaster, bamboo, cistus, lonicera, grasses and pampas are blotted with patches of bare earth.

Hampshire County Architects/Pearson Landscape Design 1997

Hackney Community College

islington and hackney

Hampshire County Architects/Pearson Landscape Design 1997

Hackney Community College

Tantalising glimpses of a number of inner courtyards through elaborate railings designed by Matthew Fedden puncture the monotony of the brick walls along Hoxton Street. One of the courtyards is home to a *Floating Stones* fountain by Lotte Glob. Another inviting outdoor room is visible from the main reception.

The campus is well-loved, and its outdoor rooms are enjoyed in all weathers. Financial investment on this scale is rare in educational, particularly higher-educational, institutions. To encourage this further, provision for after-care as well as good design is needed.

ADDRESS Shoreditch Campus, Falkirk Street, London N1
CLIENT Hackney Community College/Shoreditch Project Team on behalf of principal funders: Further Education Funding Council, Dalston City Partnership, European Regional Development Fund, Hackney Community College, London Borough of Hackney, Sports Council Lottery
CONTRACT VALUE £270,000 phase 3 landscape contract works only)
SIZE 2.95 hectares
TUBE Old Street
ACCESS by appointment (020 7613 9019), and as part of Open House scheme

Hampshire County Architects/Pearson Landscape Design 1997

Hackney Community College

islington and hackney

Hampshire County Architects/Pearson Landscape Design 1997

Period Gardens, Geffrye Museum

Continuing the impetus of the twentieth-century wing designed by Branson Coates Architecture (1998), the Geffrye Museum has created a series of new period gardens. In addition to presenting the changing style of the domestic interior, you can now see the changing styles of the domestic garden. A brick path walks the visitor through a series of middle-class town gardens, each one designed to complement its interior counterpart. It begins with a Tudor Knot Garden (late 1550s). This is followed by gardens representing the late Elizabethan era (1550–1620), the mid- to late-Georgian era (1760–1800), and the mid- to late-Victorian era (1860–90), culminating with the Edwardian era (1900–14). Like the long almshouse, the linear nature of the space lends itself to this treatment. Sadly you can't look from one to the other as this would have meant punching holes in the rear façade of the grade 1-listed building.

Metal gates and railings designed and smithied by Terence Clerk are inspired by vegetative forms. Make sure you visit the new restaurant orientated to overlook the garden, where John Creed's standard lamps begin to blur the boundary between building and garden.

The garden, maintained by the in-house team, is in its early days and the hedges will take a while to create the structure the garden rooms need. Each one will be allowed to change should further information come to light during on-going research.

ADDRESS The Geffrye Museum, Kingsland Road, London E2
CLIENT Geffrye Museum Trust
SIZE 0.1 hectare
TUBE Old Street
ACCESS open April to October

Christine Lalumia 1999

islington and hackney

Christine Lalumia 1999

tower hamlets and newham

Helling Street Play Area

Wandering along the narrow confines of Wapping High Street in the shadow of tall converted yuppie-houses, this colourful playground comes as quite a surprise. Essentially a London square, it was created as part of the new residential development that surrounds it and, like Sumner Park (see page 8.30), is predominantly devoted to play.

The square is divided into four zones. A sandy gravel path leads straight through the centre of a grove of Scots pine. Their crooked shapes make the regimental lines they are planted in less apparent. Views to the next zone are restricted to a narrow opening in a long blockwork wall, rendered and painted a brilliant cobalt blue. The pines and fading wall suggest a touch of Barcelona.

Beyond the wall, the sandy path is continued as a rubberised play surface in the same hue. This zone is dominated by a colourful synthetic hillocky landscape with a chute, slide, fort and tower bridge. It looks like a tasteful swirly carpet that's been rucked up in places – a robust and inventive alternative to the traditional grass hill and slide. The inspiration came from a painting by Lynn Kinnear's sister. Hedges on either side of the square ride over the humps but are proving tricky to establish.

In the foreground a play net, glass-reinforced rocks and timber swings are laid out on bark mulch. A five-a-side court beyond this provides a play area for older children. The galvanised railings that enclose the square are intentionally less conspicuous than traditional playground boundaries. Once the London plane trees planted outside the square mature it will be even more see-through. One of Lynn Kinnear's over-riding concerns is that demarcating areas for children's play excludes them from the world outside.

Helling Street has been widely acclaimed, and rightly so. It represents a move towards encouraging less prescriptive types of play. But play areas

Kinnear Landscape Architects 1995

tower hamlets and newham

Kinnear Landscape Architects 1995

are by definition prescriptive. In the present climate, where parents are increasingly unwilling to let their children out of sight, the question of how to provide creative play opportunities becomes more and more pertinent. Let the debate continue.

ADDRESS Helling Street, London E1
CLIENT London Docklands Development Corporation (LDDC)
ENGINEER Techniker
CONTRACT VALUE £320,000
SIZE 0.25 hectare
TUBE Wapping
ACCESS open

Kinnear Landscape Architects 1995

tower hamlets and newham

Kinnear Landscape Architects 1995

Mile End Park

Roughly 1.6km long and only 100 metres wide in some places, Mile End Park is formed from a series of Second World War bomb sites and one of Abercrombie's original 'green lungs' for London. The park runs north to south parallel with the east side of the Grand Union Canal. There are weak links at both the northern (Victoria Park) and southern (Limehouse Basin) ends where the LCC (later GLC) never managed to acquire the necessary land. It is also chopped up by three major roads and two railways. The borough of Tower Hamlets is one of the most depressed in London. By the early 1990s the park had become a no-go area after dark, used for anti-social pastimes and dog walking.

Community Land Use (CLU), a local environment agency, came up with the idea of transforming it into a 'people's park' fit for the twenty-first century. Initial overtures made to the Millennium Commission led to the formation of the Mile End Partnership (MEP) with Tower Hamlets Council and East London Partnership. The original concept to create miles of sport, art and fun reflects current thinking that inner-city parks should be full of life and activity.

Buzzwords and catchphrases like, 'sustainable', 'high quality', 'community involvement', 'regional regeneration effect' and 'completing the Abercrombie plan' were floated around. Initial consultation began in 1995, but had to be speeded up to satisfy the Millennium Commission's insistence that there should be a masterplan at bid stage. As a result Tibbalds Monroe quickly drew up a masterplan that subdivided the park into a number of activity areas, linked by a sinuous undulating path for pedestrians and cyclists.

Few Londoners can have failed to hear of the first phase, thanks to a great PR campaign. By clever manipulation of levels and views Piers Gough's Green Bridge romantically continues the park over the busy Mile

Tibbalds tmz/LB Tower Hamlets/Community Land Use 1995–

tower hamlets and newham

Tibbalds tmz/LB Tower Hamlets/Community Land Use 1995–

End Road. Large Himalayan birch trees (*Betula jacquemontii*), black pines (*Pinus nigra*) and Weymouth pines (*Pinus strobus*) are planted on top in vast containers, tied to a concrete layer below. The bridge's yellow underbelly is deliberately scooped up on either side to reduce the dark environment underneath. A concrete deck floats above the yellow soffit, providing a servicing void the height of a man. It's overlaid with polystyrene, geotextile and well-compacted soil. This fail-safe engineering solution cost a mere £500,000.

The Terrace Garden to the south of the Green Bridge is also part of phase 1 but less well advertised. It's designed for older people, particularly those in the social housing opposite. There are terraces planted with perennials and roses, reflective pools and a fountain.

The Ecology Park and the Arts Park (phase 2) lie to the north of the Green Bridge and were being built at time of writing. Each will have a new pavilion over which the serpentine footpath (and park) will rise, a wangle to get round the park's Metropolitan Land status which prohibits buildings. The buildings are designed to maximise efficiency using 'annual passive heatstore technology'. This involves keeping the soil around the building dry (to a depth of 6 metres) so that heat stored up over the summer can be slowly released back into the building in winter. The canal will be visually drawn into the park with lakes that also provide some much-needed security.

The play parks are being left until phase 3, due to start soon. The play arena to the north of the Ecology Park will have a small football area and an earth-embanked arena for spectators. To the south a staffed adventure playground will be for 10–20-year-olds. Further south (beyond the DLR line), Xtreme Sport will cater for rollerbladers, BMX bikes and skateboarders. It's hoped that Electric Karts (a business concession) will bring

tower hamlets and newham

Tibbalds tmz/LB Tower Hamlets/Community Land Use 1995–

in revenue. The Children's Park for under-10s will have a crèche. The Sports Park is the subject of a separate sports lottery bid. Mile End Stadium is to be refurbished and a new swimming pool built.

The masterplan is very rigid despite the serpentine path and Green Bridge. The themed areas reinforce the park as a series of separate entities as opposed to a continuous 'green lung'. The link to Victoria Park also remains unfulfilled. The idea that people (let alone wildlife) will use each space exactly as intended is naïve. Vandalism suggests that the consultation work failed to reach some members of the community, despite the three to four permanently employed members on the community liaison team. The level of maintenance required in each zone is intentionally high. Funding has dried up at the present time and Tower Hamlet's horticultural department is already struggling as phase 1 is handed over. A big question mark hangs over the intended park-ranger programme and to date there's still no management plan. An uncertain future lies ahead for Mile End Park.

Britain's urban parks urgently need investment but, as lottery projects begin to be examined minutely, there's a possibility that one of the first and most high-profile projects has not helped the cause.

ADDRESS Mile End Park, London E3
CLIENT Mile End Park Partnership
ENERGY AND SERVICES CONSULTANT Fulcrum Consulting
STRUCTURAL ENGINEER Mott Macdonald
CONTRACT VALUE £25 million SIZE 38.4 hectares
TUBE Mile End
ACCESS open

Tibbalds tmz/LB Tower Hamlets/Community Land Use 1995–

Tibbalds tmz/LB Tower Hamlets/Community Land Use 1995–

Canary Wharf

Thanks to the Jubilee Line extension that opened in 1999, Canary Wharf is only 15 minutes away from Waterloo and much easier to visit than ever before. Its history begins in the 1980s, with the rise of Olympia and York, a North American developer making the most of cheap land prices and relaxed building restrictions in the London Docklands Enterprise Zone. Despite their formula of buying cheap land (for which they paid 2 per cent of going rates in the City) and building speedily and innovatively, they do not build cheaply. This is the closest you'll get to streets paved with gold, Dick Whittington.

To their credit, one third of the total development area is dedicated to public open space – landscape architects, predominantly Hanna/Olin, have been involved from the start. Never far from view (and also visible from the M25), the landmark tower of 1 Canada Square has made one of the most substantial impacts on the landscape of London at the end of the twentieth century.

The masterplan by Skidmore, Owings & Merrill, advised by Sir Roy Strong, provides a network of open spaces knitted together by a strong east–west axis on the centre-wall alignment of the old dock. Its structure is formal and grandiose. A series of ornamental roof gardens and tree-lined boulevards (suspended over four-storey concrete bunkers for cars and services) provide places to stroll and relax. It's often criticised for its cars and for its lack of space for more active outdoor activities.

Phase 1 includes West Ferry Circus, a glorified roundabout designed as a traditional garden square with planting by Sir Roy Strong; West India Avenue, a leafy boulevard with 35–50-year-old lime and plane trees; Cabot Square, another traffic island, raised above the vehicles with noisy fountains by Richard Chaix, CMS, and enclosed by pleached limes; and Wren Landing with benches by Rod Wales, a small square off Cabot

Skidmore, Owings & Merrill/Hanna/Olin and others 1990–

Skidmore, Owings & Merrill/Hanna/Olin and others 1990–

Square with a temporary boules pit. SOM designed all the street furniture, including telephone booths, bus stops, litter bins and park benches.

With the completion of phase 2 there are two exciting new places to visit. Canada Square Park (the main park by Hanna/Olin, the surrounding hard landscape by Koetter Kim Associates) provides a welcome area of grass and is designed to read from the tower as a colourful abstract rug. The rug has two powerful stripes of chestnut trees woven into one edge and a sinuous path through a woodland grove stitched into the other. Annuals in square black planters appear as randomly scattered, brightly coloured, geometric shapes. The giant blue blob in the centre is Ron Arad's *Big Blue*, a sculptural skylight for the shopping mall below. It's worth visiting the shopping mall just to see an inverted image of the whole park reflected in its underbelly. The scheme is exquisitely executed and the palette of pink and grey granite provides continuity with the rest of Canary Wharf.

By contrast, Columbus Courtyard is totally paved, relieved only by its fountains and silver lime trees. The artist Igor Mitoraj conceived it as an Italian piazza setting for his giant mask sculpture. The turquoise screen by Wendy Ramshaw disguises a main approach road that passes underneath. The diode lighting by Spears and Major set into the paving adds a sparkly quality at night, an important feature since it's surrounded by banks working around the clock.

It was always intended that public art should play a major role. Throughout the Canary Wharf estate, you will see ornamental features ranging from iron railings to richly textured glass screens and large elaborate fountains, by leading artists and designers. Potentially bitty, the landscape masterplan provides a distinct framework within which the *objets d'art* help to relieve its corporate character. Several major new

Skidmore, Owings & Merrill/Hanna/Olin and others 1990–

Skidmore, Owings & Merrill/Hanna/Olin and others 1990–

works include Ron Arad's £50 million *Windwand*, and two 'sound' benches with recordings of reminiscences of the area by local people at Canary Riverside; also *Six Public Clocks* at Nash Courtyard by Konstantin Grcic.

Canary Wharf refuses to stand still. Jubilee Park, designed by the Belgian landscape architect, Pieter Wirtz (scheduled for completion in 2002) is a particularly exciting prospect. Sir Geoffrey Jellicoe famously criticised phase 1 as 'competent, self-centred, out-of-date Beaux Arts design' (*Landscape Design*, November 1991). I wonder what he would say today?

ADDRESS Canary Wharf, London E14
CLIENT Olympia and York Canary Wharf Ltd
SIZE 28.5 hectares
TUBE/DLR Canary Wharf
ACCESS open

Skidmore, Owings & Merrill/Hanna/Olin and others 1990–

Skidmore, Owings & Merrill/Hanna/Olin and others 1990–

Newcastle Drawdock

Newcastle Drawdock dates from the 1850s and has grade II-listed status for its contribution to Docklands' heritage. On the north side of the Thames and designated a conservation area, it has fine views to the Royal Naval College and the Maritime Museum at Greenwich.

The project involved the renewal of pedestrian and traffic highways, including the river walkway and seating areas adjacent to the dock. Grenville Davey (winner of the Turner Prize, 1992) was chosen from the six artists put forward to collaborate on the project by The Public Art and Development Trust. Local residents were also consulted.

The river, the walkway, the drawdock and the adjacent park are opened up. The design revolves around a centrally placed button, all based on Davey's 1988 *Button* sculpture. Low square concrete blocks emerge from the drawdock, laid out in a geometric grid on a surface of resin bonded gravel. The central blocks are linked with a carpet of galvanised steel, 'their reflective surface a continuation of the water' (*Time Out*, 18–25 August, 2000). Furniture surrounding the square includes galvanised-steel seating topped with oak; chunky galvanised railings and lighting surround the drawdock. A circular paving feature collects rainwater (intentionally). Alder trees emerge from granite setts.

The scheme is more of a public-art solution than a landscape one and may look dated quite quickly.

ADDRESS Newcastle Drawdock, Isle of Dogs, London E14
CLIENT London Docklands Development Corporation
CONTRACT VALUE £500,000
DLR Island Gardens/Cutty Sark via Greenwich foot tunnel
ACCESS open

EDAW (Tate Hopkins) 1997

EDAW (Tate Hopkins) 1997

Aberfeldy Millennium Green

This is the first Millennium Green to be completed in London. The scheme was set up by the Countryside Agency in 1996 (applications closed in 1998) with the aim of creating 250 greens by June 2001. The local community has to come up with funding to match a 50 per cent grant from the Millennium Commission Lottery Fund. Each green is protected by a thousand-year covenant.

In the case of Aberfeldy, the borough of Tower Hamlets donated the triangular plot to the local community. Community Land Use (CLU), a community-orientated practice which specialises in consultation funded by the Environment Agency (see also Mile End Park, page 6.6), acted as facilitators. The project involved extensive ground remodelling, laying Breedon gravel paths and building a very substantial brick amphitheatre, with a millennium sundial painted on its floor by local community artist David Bratby. Most of the trees and shrubs are native and were planted by local school children and British Conservation Trust Volunteers.

Surrounded by roads on all three sides, the green is rather isolated but it does provide a welcome patch of verdure. It's up to the local residents to look after it. When I visited, it needed a good weed but it's still too early to judge it fairly.

ADDRESS Aberfeldy Street, London E14
CLIENT Aberfeldy Millennium Green Trust
CONTRACT VALUE £50,000
SIZE 0.4 hectare approximately
TUBE Canning Town, then short bus ride or walk
DLR All Saints/East India Dock
ACCESS open

Aberfeldy Millennium Green Trust/Community Land Use 2000

Bow Creek Ecology Park

Sandwiched between East India Dock Road (A13) and Lower Lea Crossing (A1020), in the shadow of the DLR flyover and the flight path for City Airport, Bow Creek peninsula is not the most obvious place to look for an ecology park. Designed as a very hands-on educational resource for school children, it focuses on the role of water in habitat management.

A large circular tank stores the water extracted by windpump from a 12-metre-deep borehole. Children can control its flow through a series of water-related habitats using sluices and a water wheel. Wheelchair-friendly bound-gravel paths and timber decks navigate you round them, demonstrating water-meadow management, reedbed filtration and willow coppicing, and the more traditional pursuits of pond dipping.

Four years on, the pump is broken, brackish water stagnates in puddles and a bloated drowned rat floats in one of the ponds. Not a place to bring kids then, even if it is still a haven for wildlife. Yet another award-winning project bites the dust – a victim of poor management, the A13 development works, and probably the 1995 London Docklands Development Commission (LDDC) hand-over. East India Dock Basin was also part of the project but is now open to the public on Sundays and bank holidays following necessary health and safety works.

ADDRESS Bow Creek Peninsula, London
CLIENT LDDC. Now managed by the Trust for Urban Ecology (TRUE) on behalf of the Lee Valley Regional Park Authority
ECOLOGIST Trust for Urban Ecology (TRUE)
CONTRACT VALUE £282,000
SIZE 2 hectares
TUBE Canning Town
ACCESS by arrangement only; telephone 020 8533 6937 (LVRPA Rangers)

Gibberd Landscape Design 1995

Gibberd Landscape Design 1995

Thames Barrier Park

In 1995 an international competition was held to design a park that would provide a catalyst for the redevelopment of this area of the Royal Docks. The multi-disciplinary consortium that won included Alain Provost of Groupe Signes, best known for Parc Citröen in Paris (another industrial riverside site). The winning design created an attractive setting for adjacent residential apartments (a planning gain which has partially funded the scheme) and a new place to enjoy the Thames and its striking Barrier. It also extended the park into vacant land north of North Woolwich Road, physically linking the river with the Royal Docks.

The area was once the site of a petrochemical plant. Clearing it up involved cleaning and capping the fill with a capillary break layer of crushed concrete and sculpting it into a 6.5-metre-high plateau stepping down to a height of 4.5 metres at the river's edge.

The central feature is a sunken 'green dock', a reference to the site's industrial past as the long-disappeared Prince Regent Dock. It provides an intimate environment for the garden laid out along its floor. Herbaceous plants arranged in lines and blocks of colour bear Provost's signature. They are interspersed with waves of yew hedging rippling towards the river. Retaining walls, 4.5 metres high, planted with lonicera (*Lonicera nitida* 'Maigrun') have already achieved an even green coat (like the furry wall-carpets popular during the 1960s). The walls are stabilised using a system called CONTEC (also used along sections of the M25 corridor) and irrigated with leaky pipe feeders at 500mm centres. Giant concrete structures provide physical full-stops at either end of the dock. At the north entrance, sheer 6-metre-high concrete walls banded with black slate are animated by 36 water jets choreographed to perform different sequences.

Nearest the south bank of the river stands a timber-deck platform and

Groupe Signes/Patel Taylor Architects/Ove Arup & Partners 2000

Groupe Signes/Patel Taylor Architects/Ove Arup & Partners 2000

6.26

a 7.5-metre-high pavilion. It's dedicated to local people killed in the two World Wars.

Giant yew buttresses around the edges will become the wings to the park's stage, integrating it with its surroundings (and apartments). A glass café in the centre continues the tradition of orangeries or ornamental greenhouses, designed in a contemporary manner. It's raised on a timber deck that hovers above the ground, offering fine views of the river and an informal stage for outdoor events. Long steel tubes (35mm) bridge the dock, allowing people to cross it. They are more like aqueducts than bridges. Graphite iron railings suggest mooring posts.

High on the plateau, trees are formally laid out in a longitudinal grid. Their names can be found stencilled on the glass walls of the café in Latin. They include Austrian pine (*Pinus nigra*), sprinkled on either side of the green dock, and three types of birches, including *Betula Jacquemontii* and *B. Ermanii*, Norway maples (*Acer platanoides* 'Globusum'), sweet gum (*Liquidamber styracifolia*), Japanese pagoda trees (*Sophora japonica*), honey locust trees (*Gleditsia triacanthos*), and feathered Hungarian oaks (*Quercus frainetto*). True to the control-freak tradition of French gardens even the wild-flower meadows are supposed to be colour themed. This will require much perseverance – at the moment they are a riot of blue and white vetch.

Provost's strong resistance to a children's play area could be interpreted in a number of ways. The London Borough of Newham has insisted on one. The strange metal cage enclosing the children's play equipment is an unfortunate compromise and looks very out of place.

Thames Barrier Park is a rare example of urban regeneration focusing on open space in advance of development. There has been a vote of confidence from the neighbouring apartments which are selling like hot cakes.

tower hamlets and newham

Groupe Signes/Patel Taylor Architects/Ove Arup & Partners 2000

tower hamlets and newham

Groupe Signes/Patel Taylor Architects/Ove Arup & Partners 2000

Thames Barrier Park

It's obvious that the park must look good to fulfil its mission – yet for the moment it's relying on the pared-down resources of the (well-intentioned) local authority. Open 24 hours a day, with the exception of the 'green dock', and without a park ranger system, it's an extremely vulnerable environment. Extension to the Docklands Light Railway is also vital.

ADDRESS North Woolwich Road, London E16
CLIENT London Development Agency
CONTRACT VALUE £7.4 million (including £2.2 million remediation)
SIZE 9.4 hectares
TUBE Canning Town, then bus
RAIL Silvertown/London City Airport, then bus or walk
ACCESS open, dawn to dusk

Groupe Signes/Patel Taylor Architects/Ove Arup & Partners 2000

tower hamlets and newham

Groupe Signes/Patel Taylor Architects/Ove Arup & Partners 2000

Stratford Regional Station

Is the setting for Wilkinson Eyre's award-winning new terminal a contender in its own right? This well-detailed public piazza does not attempt to out-do its colossal neighbour but rather to complement it and offer a safe platform from which to admire it. Free from clutter (almost to the extent of sterility) only high-quality materials will do. There are granite benches and slim lighting columns the height of the new station. With time, the large ash trees will add character to the space. A twisted town clock is the only other point of interest.

Once again the scheme is let down, down, down, by lack of maintenance. A scorched-earth policy appears to be in operation for the trees and shrubs planted on along the main approach, damaging the first impressions that the building seeks to induce.

Art 2 Architecture has gained planning permission for three new squares in Stratford to be built during 2001. They intend to link the public space around the newly refurbished Theatre Royal and create a safe yet dynamic environment for Stratford's emerging quarter (*Building Design*, 14 April, 2000). This time, please think ahead.

ADDRESS Gibbons Road, London E15
CLIENT London Underground Ltd – Jubilee Line Extension Project
STRUCTURAL AND SERVICES ENGINEER Hyder Consulting
CIVIL ENGINEER Ove Arup & Partners
TUBE/DLR/RAIL Stratford
ACCESS open

Hyder Consulting 1999

The Green

Plans to upgrade the University of East London's Stratford campus so that it's not completely upstaged by the new campus on Royal Albert Dock (see page 6.34) could take from two to ten years to implement, depending on funding. As an interim measure, the university has taken the unusual step of making some temporary environmental improvements. The Green – an old car park tucked between a late-twentieth-century tower block and an Arts and Crafts working men's college dating from the 1890s – is now reclaimed for pedestrians.

The scheme provides a brazenly geometrical response to the existing buildings, only relieved by its 'soft' furnishings. A diagonal cross route (picked out in stone setts) interrupts the alternate rhythm of rectilinear strips of lawn and shrub beds, avoiding confrontation with an existing desire line. Hardwood railway sleepers elevate the shrub beds, planted with laurustinus, ceanothus, ivy, variegated iris and some white poplar trees (*Populus alba*) in the southern sections. There are duck-egg-stained timber benches built into the retaining walls. Surrounding areas, including Green Street, are coated with gravel chippings. Galvanised bollard lighting and litter bins reflect the area's historic industrial associations.

The scheme is designed to be dismantled – almost all of the parts can be sold back to suppliers, and were selected for this purpose. A temporary if expensive solution, it brings some homogeneity to the disparate collection of university buildings.

ADDRESS University of East London, Stratford, London E15
CLIENT University of East London
CONTRACT VALUE £115,500 SIZE 0.2 hectare
TUBE/DLR/RAIL Stratford
ACCESS open

Livingstone Eyre Associates 1998

Livingstone Eyre Associates 1998

University of East London

From a distance, the brightly coloured tom-tom residence halls (by Edward Cullinan Architects) in this windswept landscape evoke Southwold beachhuts more than the images of St Mark's Square, Venice, originally presented to the client. It comprises buildings grouped around a series of interlinked open spaces and goes some way to providing shelter without turning its back on the Olympic rowing dock.

The university forecourt is the most sheltered space, partly due to its sunken nature, and partly to the curved cobbled enclosures. The view to University Square is compromised by the overhang of the roundabout that circles above the station. At the heart of the campus, the colonnaded Square looks towards a raised lawn and over the dock to City Airport opposite. Bright white reconstituted paving glares back at you in sunlight. You can walk along the dock edge to the residential drums, or take a more sheltered tree-lined route along University Street. Circular lawns are edged with lavender, hazel and Portugal laurel (*Prunus lusitanica*).

The light-hearted treatment has created a distinctive landmark at the eastern extremity of the dock. Sadly, the sustainable approach to the architecture is not mirrored in the landscape. Still, the university's commitment to offering training facilities to local estate residents makes it the most public-spirited Docklands venture to date.

ADDRESS London Docklands Campus, Albert Dock, London E16
CLIENT University of East London
CONTRACT VALUE £33 million, phase 1
SIZE 6 hectares of 10-hectare site, phase 1
DLR Cyprus Station
ACCESS open

Edward Cullinan Architects/Livingstone Eyre Associates 1999

tower hamlets and newham

Edward Cullinan Architects/Livingstone Eyre Associates 1999

barnet, brent and camden

News of Venus

Pressure from the Willesden Forum and Chapel End Tenants & Residents Association (CETRA) led to a scheme to clean up a messy corner site and create an enjoyable place and a local landmark. It's one of three projects funded by the Harlesden City Challenge 'Art in the City' initiative over a five-year period, aimed at improving the local environment. Lord Learie Constantine Park, Villiers Road and Villa Altamira at the junction of Brentfield Road with Hillside were designed by the same team at a similar time. Despite the pigeon problem, News of Venus is the best maintained, highlighting the futility of schemes without adequate provision.

The landmark, a 2.5-metre-high steel totem pole by Geraldine Konyn (Jelly Wall Productions), is decorated with images reflecting the borough's multicultural mix. It weighs a ton and cost £3000. Concrete seats radiate from it with curved, galvanised steel support rails. The points of the compass are marked in stainless-steel lettering on concrete sitting blocks. A series of gentle stepped ramps and paths paved with Blanc de Bièrge rconcrete setts ationalise the change in levels and allow wheelchair access.

The issue of public art is a constant challenge. Art should not be viewed as a magic wand that can somehow solve the social and physical problems of a site. Here, artist and landscape architect have clearly worked together.

ADDRESS junction of Willesden High Road with Dudden Hill Lane, London NW10
CLIENT London Borough of Brent
CONTRACT VALUE £50,000
TUBE Neasden/Dollis Hill/Willesden Green
ACCESS open

barnet, brent and camden

Brent Environmental Services 1993

The Pergola, The Hill Garden

The grade-II listed raised pergola walk is as long as Canary Wharf is tall (244 metres) and is part of The Hill Garden designed by Thomas H Mawson, first president of the Landscape Institute. It was built over a 20-year period (1906–15) and designed to screen Lord Leverhulme's house (now known as Inverforth House) from his kitchen garden and from people walking on West Heath.

The 8-metre-high retaining walls were constructed using excavated spoil from the extension of the Northern Line to Hampstead. The last extension to the long colonnade includes a belvedere with views to Harrow on the Hill, more than 10 kilometres away. There are photographs of the pergola in its heyday in Mawson's book, *The Art and Craft of Garden Making*.

In 1963, The Hill Garden (including the pergola) was separated from the house and opened to the public. By the time the Corporation of London took control the pergola was in such a state of disrepair that it had begun to slide down the hill. An intensive restoration programme followed. The south-west corner has been completely rebuilt. Its orientation is altered in places to block views to the gardens – recently restored by J & L Gibbons – which now belong to the upmarket apartments in Inverforth House.

The former kitchen garden at the foot of the pergola is also open to the public, its geometrical layout broadly based on Mawson's original plan. A tasteful selection of trees, shrubs and perennials, including apple trees, artichokes and an assortment of herbs, is intended to give the gardens a culinary flavour. The remnants of old greenhouses have been oddly incorporated into the scheme and a terraced area is still used for standing out sub-tropical plants in summer. The intention is to provide more climbers for the pergola and to add seating.

Corporation of London/Gareth Stansfield 1995

The Pergola, The Hill Garden

The Pergola, The Hill Garden

The pergola makes the transition between tamed, manicured gardens and the wilderness of the heathland elegant once more.

The rest of The Hill Garden should now be tackled. Here, the undulating lawns, lily pond and informal tree and shrub borders to the north of the pergola (also designed by Mawson) are in a less healthy state of repair. The restored pergola accentuates the contrast and in many ways disassociates itself.

ADDRESS Inverforth Close, North End Way, London NW3
CLIENT Corporation of London
CONTRACT VALUE £1.3 million
TUBE Hampstead/Golders Green; entrance off Inverforth Close or path off North End Way (A502)
ACCESS open 9.00–dusk

Corporation of London/Gareth Stansfield 1995

Corporation of London/Gareth Stansfield 1995

British Library Forecourt

The library is set well back from Euston Road. Enclosing walls create a vast entrance courtyard which is dominated by Eduardo Paolozzi's giant bronze figure of Newton. The arched brick gateway is positioned at the opposite corner of the square to the main entrance doors. Visitors are encouraged to cross the piazza on a diagonal, for the best view of the building.

The library and forecourt are designed as a set piece. In keeping with the internal treatment, surfaces are designed to be multi-functional with 'varied surfaces on which to sit, balconies on which to lean, short flights of steps (and escalators), and visually breaking up large expanses of floor surface through a grid pattern in the stone and brick paving' (S Hardingham, *London: a guide to recent architecture*, 1999).

The token amphitheatre (why is a scheme incomplete without one?) conflicts with this philosophy, and, if we're being picky, the red brickwork (from the same stock in Leicestershire as St Pancras Chambers) is slightly overwhelming. I would like to have seen a few more trees! But the forecourt boasts its own outdoor café and provides a welcome retreat from the busy Euston Road.

ADDRESS 96 Euston Road, London NW1
CLIENT The British Library Board
ENGINEER Ove Arup & Partners
TUBE Euston/King's Cross
ACCESS open Monday, Wednesday to Friday, 9.30–18.00; Tuesday, 9.30–20.00; Saturday, 9.30–17.00, Sunday, 11.00–17.00

Colin St John Wilson and Partners 1997

British Library Forecourt

Colin St John Wilson and Partners 1997

lambeth and southwark

Bonnington Square

This deceptively small communal garden is a little gem. Its success is due to the commitment of local residents. Initial overtures were made to the borough of Lambeth to convert a bit of leftover tarmac with some swings. The residents – a collection of filmmakers and artists, including the well-known garden designer, Dan Pearson – qualified for a Voluntary Environment Improvement Programme grant. Lambeth allowed them to help with the design and even implement the planting. Whitelaw Turkington administered the grant and assisted with key aspects of the design.

The entrance pergola, crowned with the hull of an old boat, frames a view to two arbours. At one end Mediterranean plants envelop a quiet sitting area, their feathery foliage complementing the spiky forms of *Chaemerops humilis*. At the opposite end, swings stand next to a mound of silver birch trees. Various sculptural bits and pieces are scattered about: the carcass of a water wheel, a rusty old chaise longue. The exposed edges of the garden are wrapped in ribbon of variegated and evergreen pittosporum hedge (*Pittosporum tenufolium*) clipped to form waves.

The spirit of the garden appears to have spread in a manner most uncharacteristic for Britain. Trees in the street are underplanted with bulbs; paving slabs removed and substituted with clusters of phormiums; climbers race up street lights; and large pots are positioned on the pavement at the entrance to a block of flats.

ADDRESS Bonnington Square, London SW8
CLIENT Bonnington Square Residents Association
CONTRACT VALUE £18,000
SIZE 0.1 hectare
TUBE Vauxhall
ACCESS open

Local Resident Trust/Whitelaw Turkington 1994

Bonnington Square

lambeth and southwark

Local Resident Trust/Whitelaw Turkington 1994

The Tibetan Peace Garden, Samten Kyil

The Tibetan name 'Samten Kyil' means place (or garden) of contemplation. The garden is a gift from the Tibetan Foundation to the people of Britain, symbolising the meeting of East and West, and representing a marriage of contemporary Western and traditional Tibetan imagery. The Tibetan Foundation hopes that it will serve to create a greater awareness of Buddhist culture. After an initial inquiry by Hamish Horsely, Southwark Council offered a site close to the Imperial War Museum. It's an apt location, albeit rather noisy, and is rather more high profile than expected.

The circular design is based on the Buddhist image of the Dharma Wheel. At the centre of the circle, set in black Kilkenny limestone, rests a bronze cast of the Kalachakra Mandala (wheel of time) designed by Tibetan monks in India and later carved in stone in the artists' studio by Tim Metcalf, Awang Dorjee and Iassen Dimitrov. At gateways on the outer perimeter of the circle positioned at the compass points stand four stylised abstractions carved in Portland stone. These portray the elements: air (west gateway), fire (north), earth (east), and water (south). The open arena represents the fifth element, space. The five elements are held in Buddhism to constitute the basis of our whole existence: environment, life and consciousness. Outside the arena is the Language Pillar on which a message for the millennium by His Holiness The Dalai Lama is carved in English, Tibetan, Chinese and Hindi.

Set into the paving around the mandala are the 'Eight Auspicious Symbols' cast in bronze: the banner of victory, golden fishes, vase of treasure, lotus, conch shell, external knowledge, parasol and wheel. Eight York stone meditation seats surround the central mandala, with herbs and plants from Tibet and Himalayan regions planted behind. White roses and the stems of white Himalayan birch (*Betula jacquemontii*),

Hamish Horsley (sculptor)/Guy Stansfeld (architect) 1996

lambeth and southwark

Hamish Horsley (sculptor)/Guy Stansfeld (architect) 1996

combined with the whiteness of the stone have further peace connotations. The layout of the paving and finely detailed oak and steel pergola give the garden a sense of unity and a contemporary edge. The outer perimeter path is laid with a (too) thick layer of gravel with crudely laid timber edging. A trust fund has been set up to assist with maintenance.

The garden is beautifully designed and executed. It is self-contained but will become more integrated with its surroundings once trees mature. Most important of all, it's a monument to the courage and resilience of the Tibetan people. Plans to restore Geraldine Mary Harmsworth Park are currently under way.

ADDRESS Geraldine Mary Harmsworth Park, St George's Road, London SE1
CLIENT Tibet Foundation
CONTRACT VALUE £400,000
TUBE Lambeth North/Elephant & Castle
ACCESS open

Hamish Horsley (sculptor)/Guy Stansfeld (architect) 1996

Hamish Horsley (sculptor)/Guy Stansfeld (architect) 1996

Members' Courtyard, County Hall

The old GLC Members' Courtyard now forms the entrance to the London Marriott Hotel. Its new layout is intended to retain the scale and grandeur, create a prestigious hotel entrance, excite curiosity, entice people from the street, and to allow circulation for taxis and pedestrians (no parking). All, of course, to the satisfaction of English Heritage.

The circular grass terraces rise like a pyramid, forming an unusual turning circle. In direct sunlight, it glistens invitingly at the end of the gloomy entrance passage. Irresistibly interactive, the hotel generously turns a blind eye to people sitting or playing 'king of the castle' games. The geometry complements the architecture that surrounds it, especially the most recent architectural addition to the building façade.

The structure is built over an arcade and designed to keep the weight down. The inside of the mound is constructed of solid polystyrene, covered with a 300mm layer of topsoil. The vertical edge of each grass step is retained with a porous hoarding (Grodan), and reinforced at the back with a metal rod fixed to metal uprights. The grass is watered and clipped by hand, and regularly fertilised to keep it looking green and lush.

ADDRESS Westminster Bridge Road, London SE1
CLIENT Whitbread Hotel Company
TUBE Waterloo
ACCESS with discretion and respect for hotel clientele

Kim Wilkie Associates 1998

Kim Wilkie Associates 1998

London Eye

This narrow public space, slipped in between the north elevation of County Hall and Jubilee Gardens, provides a semi-formal approach to the London Eye (by Marks Barfield Architects). Like the wheel, it's stylish, functional and robust; unlike it, the scheme relies on natural materials rather than technology.

The central area divides into a series of sunken landings and granite steps, designed to impede terrorists in white vans. A café and ticket kiosk act as an informal gateway to the wheel. Large granite cubes work as bollards, seating, and fence posts. Pairs of cubes along the north boundary are offset by a very long granite bench and yew hedging. To the south, a wide, formally planted border softens the stone of the County Hall balustrade. An avenue of double-flowering cherry trees (*Prunus avium* 'Plena') encourages people to queue in an orderly line.

Cotswold gravel was chosen as a cheap material to absorb the noise of thousands of feet. Redolent of Parisian boulevards and Copenhagen's Tivoli Gardens, British contractors struggled to lay it correctly. Teething problems were still unresolved at the time of writing.

An extended Jubilee Gardens is central to architect Rick Mather's masterplan for the South Bank.

ADDRESS Jubilee Gardens, London SE1
CLIENT British Airways London Eye
TUBE Waterloo
ACCESS open

Edward Hutchison Landscape Architects 2000

Edward Hutchison Landscape Architects 2000

Spine Route Improvements, South Bank

The South Bank stretches from Lambeth Bridge to Blackfriars Bridge and south to The Cut. The legacy of the Festival of Britain (1951), it remains a poorly connected hotchpotch of buildings, unresolved open spaces and barren car parks. It can look depressing and squalid. Commercial and political pressures have stifled progress. Most Londoners expect more from the capital's cultural centre.

While the architectural profession (Terry Farrell, Richard Rogers, and now Rick Mather) continue to come up with masterplans, the people who live and work there are not prepared to wait any longer. They have formed the South Bank Employer's Group (SBEG, 1995) and are starting to take direct action (inspired by Coin Street Community Builders). This involves slowly implementing a wish-list of projects identified in the Urban Design Strategy prepared by Llewelyn Davies and Imagination in 1994, following a traffic and pedestrian study by Ove Arup & Partners in 1993.

The improvement to Belvedere Road and Upper Ground Road – a stretch of road that runs behind the river front between Hungerford and Blackfriars Bridges – is the first environmental project to be tackled. Nobody owned this stretch so no one took responsibility for it. Cars parked everywhere; the needs of residents and pedestrians were ignored. It had become a street that buildings turned their backs on and a dumping ground for street furniture. Lifschutz Davidson have reconceived the street as a linear business park. The road is narrowed in favour of wide pedestrian-friendly pavements. The speed limit is reduced to 20 miles per hour and broad speed bumps provide at-grade crossings. A common pavement surface of resin-bonded gravel (Clearmac) unites the buildings (their private curtilage plotted in metallic studs), with red asphalt for the roads. An avenue of honey locust trees (*Gleditsia triacanthos* 'Skyline')

Lifschutz Davidson 1997

Spine Route Improvements, South Bank

Lifschutz Davidson 1997

Spine Route Improvements, South Bank

provides a green spine. Colourful banners add height to this vertical spine. Street lights are mounted on the same poles. Street furniture is restricted to a palette of stainless-steel bollards, bins, and cycle stands.

SBEG members contribute to a management fund to supplement work undertaken by the local authority, including a daily patrol of the area, cleaning signs and posting monthly updates about events and activities. Lifschutz Davidson claim they are three-fifths of the way to turning a 'rat run into a tree-lined boulevard'. There is still some clutter and it's a shame a creative alternative to the double yellow lines could not be found.

Funding was negotiated from 22 sources, including the government's SRB, the local council, the National Lottery Fund and local business. Future projects include a scheme called Waterloo Place to improve pedestrian access to station at grade and create a new pedestrian square in front of Victory Arch; a cross-river public transport system; a phased programme to upgrade the riverside walkway; an 'eco-bus' linking Covent Garden with the South Bank, Bankside and London Bridge; and new footbridges on either side of Hungerford Bridge.

Also see improvements to the spaces around the National Theatre by Stanton Williams Partnership, in particular Theatre Square; and Esso Downstream garden forecourt by BUJ architects.

ADDRESS Upper Ground and Belvedere Road, London SE1
CLIENT South Bank Employers Group
LANDSCAPE PLANNER Jeremy Lever
TRAFFIC AND HIGHWAYS ENGINEER The Denis Wilson Partnership
CONTRACT VALUE £5 million
TUBE Waterloo/Southwark
ACCESS open

Lifschutz Davidson 1997

lambeth and southwark

Lifschutz Davidson 1997

Tate Modern

In contrast to some Millennium projects, the British press has proclaimed the new Tate a triumph. Visitor numbers are far exceeding expectations and targets. Herzog + de Meuron have succeeded in creating an art powerhouse fit for the twenty-first century and the world's biggest gallery.

Bankside Power Station was built by Sir Giles Gilbert Scott in 1955, at the centre of what was then London's industrial heartland. By the 1970s the docks were redundant and industry had moved downstream. The power station closed in 1981, after 20 years of service. Artists seeking cheap studio space began to colonise this forgotten zone of abandoned warehouses. In 1994 the Tate took the bold decision to house its modern-art collection in the power station. An international competition was held and the then-little-known Swiss architects Herzog + de Meuron were commissioned to undertake the conversion.

Most of the budget was spent converting the building and applying solid design principles in a formal and clinical but low-key manner. Herzog + de Meuron were insistent that the external spaces should echo the inside ones. Unfortunately, much of the landscape budget was quickly eaten up underground, dealing with unrecorded power cables.

Approaching the Tate from the Thames, rectangular bosques of birch-trees contained with steel edging channel views to and from the building. Birch were selected as fast-growing, disease-resistant and robust trees, but it will take a while before they make any real impact. The aim is to form an arch out of the avenue along the main approach path. On the south side of the building, dogwood, quince and crab-apple hedging will be clipped at different heights to form an inward-facing green amphitheatre. The grass lawns contain squares of bulbs waiting to erupt in spring.

There are still teething problems to be resolved. The gravel paths are proving hard to maintain given the quantity of visitors (chewing gum is

Kienast Vogt Associates/Charles Funke Associates 2000

Kienast Vogt Associates/Charles Funke Associates 2000

a particular problem). Charles Funke Associates admit that grass is not the ideal surface in these circumstances, but it was particularly requested by local residents. The Tate's non-authoritarian image does not allow for 'keep off' notices. The floodwall removal and erection of new railings set off some alarm bells but it's now setting the precedent for treatment elsewhere along this stretch of the river.

The scheme feels temporary (birch is a pioneer species, after all) but its designers would argue that this is deliberate. The problems are a reminder that landscape takes time to perform, unlike the precise science of architecture. Like it or hate it, it's an exciting set piece that should inspire discussion and debate and, like most of the schemes in this book, should be judged over time.

ADDRESS Bankside, London SE1
CLIENT Tate Gallery of Modern Art
ENGINEERS Ove Arup & Partners
CONTRACT VALUE £4.5 million (of which
£500,000 soft landscape)
TUBE Southwark
ACCESS open

Kienast Vogt Associates/Charles Funke Associates 2000

Kienast Vogt Associates/Charles Funke Associates 2000

Bankside

Architects have carried out various environmental improvements to the streets that lie in the area rebranded as Bankside, between Blackfriars and London Bridge, to improve the lot of the pedestrian. Access to the area has never been better, thanks to the extension of the Jubilee Line. It's also (in theory) just a five-minute stroll from St Paul's Cathedral and the City over the Millennium Bridge.

Pioneering planner Fred Manson (head of development and regeneration at Southwark Council) is keen to reinforce the area's identity without going down the road of Victorian lamp posts and matching litter bins. A £3.65 million Southwark Design Initiative was launched in conjunction with the Architectural Foundation. Rather than commission one designer to 'play God', a handful of practices were asked to give ideas for upgrading streets and to identify new links.

'BANKSIDE' in huge lettering by Caruso St John is splurged across five sites, fuelling charges of rebranding. Materials include shiny stainless steel fixed to a lime-stained, brick railway arch wall and timber (tropical hardwood) attached to the river floodwall below the Tate, visible at low tide. The street signs highlighting key pedestrian routes across Bankside with enamelled signs and finger posts in shot-blasted cast aluminium are more understated.

East Architects' contribution involved treating the pavements of Borough High Street and Green Dragon Court with asphalt (mastic), which seems to be very popular with architects these days. It was chosen for its cheapness and easy-to-lay quality. Polished Italian terrazzo doormats have the name of each establishment picked out in stainless steel. The asphalt provides a neutral background for the doormats. Spongy rubber mats mark public facilities such as telephone booths. East also suggested paving the route from Southwark station to the Tate with grey

various designers 1996–

various designers 1996–

limestone, and lining it with angled mirrors on poles to provide views of the railway viaducts nearly.

Southwark Street is a narrow canyon, blackened by exhaust fumes with booming traffic. Muf architects began by producing a video of local residents voicing over '100 desires for Southwark Street'. A pilot scheme, which has been hyped beyond belief, is implemented at the end of Thrale Street. A black polished-concrete bench with an inset white seat at a child-friendly level and logos by local children points in the direction of the Tate. There's another custom-made white concrete bench along Southwark Street – now a subtle shade of 'dirty white'. The pavement has been widened 'as if the shore of the Thames had turned inland' and laid with panels of in situ exposed aggregate concrete. Muf are also busy 'greening' the area, encouraging local businesses and residents to plant up window boxes, funded by the council.

Patel Taylor Architects have been commissioned to remodel a section of the Riverside Walk along Bankside Road between the Tate and the Globe theatre. A cantilevered timber walkway will broaden the riverside path, projecting over the Thames and creating a new vantage point from which to view St Paul's.

At London Bridge, Eric Parry Associates' Southwark Needle, a 16-metre tapering tower of Portland stone at 19.5 degrees, remembers the old medieval gateway and points to Southwark Cathedral. Groundwork Southwark, in their first project, have improved the pedestrian walkway under Southwark Bridge with a series of carved slate panels depicting frost fairs on the frozen Thames.

The overall effect is intentionally piecemeal, characteristic of the bottom-up regeneration approach that's in vogue at the moment. English Heritage has shown its concern by commissioning Kim Wilkie Associates

various designers 1996–

Bankside

to undertake an urban strategy. It's not easy. Along with the Globe, Tate Modern has more than succeeded in raising Bankside's profile. The charm of the area is in its disparate parts, its seedy alleyways, the juxtaposition of old, very old and new. An inevitable tide of development threatens to destroy it. Remove the forgotten backstreets and you will remove the vitality that brought the new attractions in the first place – proceed with care.

ADDRESS Southwark Street (junction with Thrale Street), Borough High Street and Green Dragon Court, Thames Riverside Walk and Clink Street, London SE1
CLIENT London Borough of Southwark
TUBE Southwark/London Bridge/Blackfriars
ACCESS open

various designers 1996–

various designers 1996–

Heart of the Park, Burgess Park

Burgess Park's chequered past begins during the 1940s. At that time it was covered by dense housing and factories sited along the Grand Surrey Canal. The area was heavily bombed in the Second World War and, as part of Lord Abercrombie's Plan for London (1943), clearance of the bomb-damaged sites began by 1951. Following the abolition of the GLC in 1985, responsibility for the park passed to the London Borough of Southwark who, by the 1990s, had acquired the remaining plots to form a continuous area of public open space. Today, it's almost 5 kilometres long and more than twice the size of St James's Park, scarred with the remnants of old roads, underlying services, and the skeletal remains of old canal bridges.

The park is probably one of Groundwork's most infamous projects in London, largely due to a history of false starts. Groundwork Southwark was set up in 1995 in specific response to a previous report on the park. Together with landscape architects EDAW, Groundwork produced a masterplan and submitted a funding bid to the Millennium Commission in 1996. The application (part of the same batch as Mile End Park, see page 6.6) was unsuccessful. Groundwork Southwark announced they would implement the masterplan slowly.

Heart of the Park provides a new entrance and two seating areas. There are amenity shrubberies, groups of fastigiate hornbeams, with avenues linking to the wider park. A low wavy wall made from yellow-stained timber sleeper uprights defines an area of longer grass and wild flowers, through which paths are mown in summer. Mosaics by Michael Farady decorate three windows on the back of an old building, framed by clematis and honeysuckle sent clambering up metal frames. It's the first scheme to be implemented and typical of Groundwork's incremental approach, but it already marks a departure from the EDAW masterplan.

Groundwork Southwark/Adams Habermehl 1998

Heart of the Park, Burgess Park

Groundwork Southwark/Adams Habermehl 1998

Heart of the Park, Burgess Park

Groundwork Southwark have also upgraded the Burgess Park to Peckham Square section of the Southwark Green Chain Walk. Sponsored by Safe Routes to School, the scheme includes a widened path, lighting and four gates designed by children. It forms a green linear park along the alignment of the Surrey Canal (filled in 1972).

ADDRESS Albany Road (corner of Wells Way), London SE5
CLIENT London Borough of Southwark
CONTRACT VALUE £300,000
SIZE 1 hectare
TUBE Elephant & Castle, then short bus ride
ACCESS open

Groundwork Southwark/Adams Habermehl 1998

lambeth and southwark

Groundwork Southwark/Adams Habermehl 1998

Sumner Park

This pocket neighbourhood park is the first of three parks (including Camden Park and Chandler Park) identified within the SRB area to receive funding. It's essentially a garden square surrounded by a recent residential development and was the subject of an urban-design competition.

Within the park, a wide timber-deck bridge bisects a central grass lawn that swims in a sea of paving. The unusual choice and combination of paving materials, in particular the glazed orange tiles, is let down by detailing and implementation. A series of blue glazed walls informally segregates the children's play area from the rest of the park. At the southern end of the park, a locked-up pavilion (by architects Architype), resembles the up-turned hull of a boat. Willow multi-stems have been planted around the perimeter of the park as a hedge. Inside, fruit trees are under-planted with aromatic herbs and perennials, including sage, fennel and artichokes.

In the absence of adequate maintenance and management, the scheme is over-ambitious. The park seems to be guilty of ignoring its surroundings in more ways than one. It's a lost opportunity and those involved could look to the enlightened housing schemes of our Dutch neighbours for inspiration.

ADDRESS Sumner Road, Peckham,
London SE15
CLIENT Peckham Partnership for London
Borough of Southwark
CONTRACT VALUE £450,000
SIZE 4 hectares
RAIL Peckham Rye
ACCESS open

Jennifer Coe Landscape Architects 1999

Jennifer Coe Landscape Architects 1999

Peckham Square

The site is at the head of the Surrey Canal linear park and cycle route leading to Burgess Park. The new square develops an idea by Fred Manson, lead planner at Southwark, who sees the square as a magnetic force rather than a formal space between buildings.

Paving is conceived as a carpet of concrete, overlaid with a grid of black and white granite strips. Sculptural spheres (by Duncan Hooson) representing the four elements emerge from the paving. Beyond the carpet are areas of natural aggregate, tarmac, woodblock and sleepers, edged with trees and wavy stainless steel benches. The carpet projects into the undercroft of Alsop and Störmer's award-winning extra-terrestrial library.

Jennifer Coe Landscape Architects designed the library zone. Yet another carpet – random stripes of Blanc de Bièrge setts laid in pale red tarmacadam – draws people towards the square; blue Jesmonite paving slabs are scattered about on top. The building is set on a mat of black cobbles.

By night, buildings light up and fibre optics bounce light off reflective glass cats' eyes pasted on the spheres, continuing a theme explored by the high-tensile barometric arch. Despite all the latest gizmos, by day it appears rather windswept and lacks homogeneity.

ADDRESS Peckham High Street, London SE15
CLIENTS Southwark Regeneration & Environment/Peckham Partnership
CONTRACT VALUE £1.2 million
RAIL Peckham Rye
ACCESS open

Southwark Building Design Services/Jennifer Coe 2000

Southwark Building Design Services/Jennifer Coe 2000

Tower Bridge Piazza

Two squares (sorry, piazzas) are linked by a narrow passageway and enclosed by four blocks housing shops, offices and apartments. Surely this high-density mixed-use development, also known as Horselydown, inspired by Italian hill towns and next door to Tower Bridge, should be a case study for the Urban Task Force? Empty shop shells tell another story.

Tony Donaldson's fountain dominates the main piazza, surrounded by fancy coloured-brick paving patterns. Whitebeam trees (*Sorbus aria*) planted in concrete rings are beginning to look tired. A few of the rings are fitted with bespoke timber seats – freestanding stainless-steel benches look like a later addition. The second square, the poor relation, benefits from the vitality generated by the Anchor Tap pub in one corner. The landscape detailing is neither hilltop town nor Shad Thames and lacks the character and sense of place of Butlers Wharf.

Locals blame tight letting agreements and failure to attract the right kind of businesses in the past. The architects might argue that the spatial dimensions are not as intended. A raised stone plinth in the main piazza masks foundations for additional shops – planning permission lapsed and pressure from local residents ensured they never happened. They would have reduced the piazza to half its size but perhaps made it more effective at poaching punters off the main drag along Shad Thames.

ADDRESS Horselydown Lane, London SE1
CLIENT Berkley House plc
CONTRACT VALUE £16.5 million
SIZE 14,200 square metres
TUBE Tower Hill, then walk over Tower Bridge/London Bridge
ACCESS open

Wickham Van Eyck 1989

Wickham Van Eyck 1989

greenwich and woolwich

Cherry Garden Pier

This linear neighbourhood park links a late-1980s housing development with the Thames. A road separates the housing from a semi-private, narrow riverside garden that steps up to the riverside walk. The garden contrasts with the riverside walk, where the same sense of ownership is less in evidence. Its elevated and exposed position offers fine views to Tower Bridge.

The riverside garden has a distinctly woodland character with birch and cherry trees underplanted with shade-tolerant shrubs including coppice willow and hazel. Narrow cobbled paths snake in and out of the trees, with niches at intervals to provide sheltered seating. Several bronze figures by Diane Gorvin depict *Dr Salter's Day Dream*. Raised platforms, steps and benches create informal play elements. Almost ten years old, it's looking a little worn round the edges, a line of willow trees have taken a battering, but it's obviously well loved and looked after. The garden looks its best in spring when daffodils are in their prime and blossom decorates the path.

ADDRESS riverside, Bermondsey Wall East, London SE16
CLIENT London Docklands Development Corporation (LDDC)
CONTRACT VALUE £300,000
TUBE Bermondsey
ACCESS open

RNJM 1991

Twinkle Park

The most unusual aspect of this refurbished neighbourhood park is the flexible galvanised gazebo at its centre. During term time the gazebo allows one half of the park to be closed, providing a playground for the adjoining school. After school and during school holidays its gates are rolled open, transforming it back into a park for the whole community. It's an innovative solution in an area renowned for its lack of open space.

Until 1992 this was a run-down local-authority playground, little more than a patch of tarmac surrounded by trees and iron railings. Today it boasts wildlife gardens and a floodlit football pitch with seating. It's the result of an impressive partnership between the council, local businesses and the local community, with funding from Creekside Single Regeneration Budget (SRB), Bridge House Estates and a Section 106 planning gain agreement (Fairview Housing Development).

The wildlife garden is open to the public all the time. Situated at the quieter end of the site, it's a charming oasis. A shallow pond (one metre deep in the centre) is surrounded by wide timber decking suitable for pond-dipping. David Ireland managed to persuade the authorities not to erect a protective rail, citing Camley Street Nature Park in King's Cross as a precedent. Oxygenating plants appear to be taking over the pond. 'Danger' is carved on the decking in a variety of languages including Yemeni, Cantonese and Somali, reflecting the area's multicultural community. Large stone boulders and marginal plants restrict access to a small number of places.

In the school playground, the grassy ridge-and-furrow landscape (designed to suggest rippling waves, complete with galvanised boat beached on a wave) was never given a chance to establish itself properly. Shrubs planted beneath existing London plane trees along the perimeter have simply worn away. Ireland says the tarmac active area that doubles

David Ireland Landscape Architects 1999

Twinkle Park

David Ireland Landscape Architects 1999

Twinkle Park

as the football pitch is a victim of its own success. However, the low curving benches that surround it seem to be standing up to the test. Maintenance is carried out by Greenwich Council, the current landowner.

The park is one of a network of three spaces to be upgraded. Stage 1, Twinkle Park, and stage 2, Benbow Street, are now completed. In stage 3 it is intended to refurbish Charlotte Turner Gardens.

ADDRESS Watergate Street, London SE8
CLIENT AND PROJECT CO-ORDINATOR Greenwich Mural Workshop
GAZEBO DESIGNERS City Arts, Nigel Abbott, Victorian Lace
CONTRACT VALUE £346,000
RAIL Deptford
DLR Greenwich
ACCESS open

David Ireland Landscape Architects 1999

David Ireland Landscape Architects 1999

Cutty Sark Gardens

Cutty Sark Gardens (1954–57) were built as part of a scheme to preserve the Cutty Sark tea clipper (and later Sir Francis Chichester's Gypsy Moth) in a dry dock. Just in time for the Millennium celebrations, Timpson Manley transformed the gardens from a desolate windswept wasteland to a lively and inviting place suitable for impromptu events and the more organised Greenwich and Docklands Arts Festival and London marathon. The scheme demonstrates how the spirit of such an historic site – recently given World Heritage status and part of West Greenwich's Conservation Area – can be captured and creatively reinterpreted for the twenty-first century.

The public open space divides into two areas, thanks to an underground car park that's only half underground. An elevated area over the car park provides a platform for enjoying the river, sitting and chatting or simply watching the world go by. Timber sitting-steps bridge down to the main thoroughfare leading to the clipper, to the foot tunnel (via Brunel's rotunda) and to Terry Farrell's new ferry terminal.

There are timber decks and boardwalks of Douglas fir. A timber screen blocks off views to an adjacent housing estate along the western edge. The screen is fitted with timber benches, interpretation panels about the history of the area, brightly coloured banners and new column and bulkhead lights. The rust-coloured finish of the rendered wall and red and green diode marker lights are reminiscent of old Thames barge sails. Car-park vents are disguised with boat-shaped benches on top. Chunky metal balustrades refer to an industrial past. Bollards designed as mini-lighthouses light up the route from Greenwich Church Street to the foot tunnel. Long-destroyed lines of streets and houses are remembered in York and Caithness stone. In light of this, the decision to lay less-robust concrete paviors along the main thoroughfare is curious.

Timpson Manley 1999

greenwich and woolwich

Timpson Manley 1999

Cutty Sark Gardens

Timpson Manley are busy elsewhere in Greenwich. They are currently leading a major £7 million refurbishment of the nearby Meridian Estate and designing wayfinding pedestrian sign systems for the town centre and covered craft market.

ADDRESS Cutty Sark Gardens, London SE10
CLIENT Greenwich Development Agency
STRUCTURAL ENGINEER Dewhurst Macfarlane and Partners
M & E Fulcrum Consulting
GRAPHIC DESIGN Liberation Design Consultants
CONTRACT VALUE £1.3 million
SIZE 1 hectare
DLR Cutty Sark for Maritime Greenwich
ACCESS open

Timpson Manley 1999

Timpson Manley 1999

Greenwich Peninsula

As all eyes focus on the fate of the Millennium Dome, the press tend to ignore what is going on elsewhere on the 119-hectare Greenwich Peninsula. Since the purchase of the former Greenwich Peninsula Gas Works in February 1997, work has been carried out at breakneck speed: 27,000 tons of contaminated tar have been cleaned on site; 12.5 kilometres of pedestrian and cycle ways have been laid; more than 12,000 trees and 60,000 shrubs have been planted; and enough turf laid for 20 football pitches.

The new landscape responds to English Partnerships' main objectives: to create an immediate setting to support the staging of the Millennium Experience and to achieve a long-term landscaped environment for a predominantly residential area. The landscape masterplan 'imagines a scenario in which the marshland of the original peninsula has been entirely transformed into a forested surface and only then has urbanisation taken place'. Spaces are carved out of the forest to form parks, greens and squares, which are heavily planted. A 7- x 7-metre geometric grid has been thrown across the peninsula to determine the position of each tree and shrub. Multiples of the number seven even determined the width of the 3.5-metre paths and 7.3-metre roads (sounds scary, but it's not so evident on the ground).

There are 20 hectares of public open space. A central spine of public parkland (2 kilometres long) runs north–south linking three of the five main areas which include Meridian Gardens, Millennium Plaza, Central Park, Southern Park and Riverside Walk. The parkland is designed as a protected corridor acknowledging the peninsula's exposure to prevailing south-west winds and north-east winter winds, opening up in places to views of the river, the Thames Barrier and Canary Wharf. The spine contains most of the pedestrian, cycle and access routes within the site.

The Meridian Gardens (73 hectares) were home to the Millennium

Richard Rogers Partnership/Devigne & Dalnoky/W S Atkins 1997

Richard Rogers Partnership/Devigne & Dalnoky/W S Atkins 1997

Experience (otherwise known as the Dome), its future still unknown a time of writing. They lie at the northern tip of the peninsula at the point where the Greenwich Meridian passes through the site. The wetland gardens – spearheaded by wildlife expert Chris Baines, the Environment Agency and English Nature – will be left as the permanent legacy of the celebrations. Temporary exhibitions designed by Dan Pearson include the Hanging Gardens (to screen Greenwich North station air vents) and a 5.5-metre-high 'living wall' of willow stretching from the Dome to the river. Rainwater from the Dome roof is filtered through the reed beds to be reused inside, making it the largest grey-water recycling project to date.

Millennium Plaza, a large square at the heart of the proposed central business district, links the station to the river's edge, and is designed to hold up to 20,000 people. Central Park forms the focus of the mid-peninsula residential quarter. The park is conceived as a series of interconnecting clearings within the 'forest'. Poplar, birch, oak, hornbeam and ash define the clearing, underplanted with ivy, which could prove a maintenance nightmare. The continuity and width of the park are compromised by the existing pub and a row of listed cottages and, more importantly, by the proposed Millennium Transit Link – Britain's first computer-controlled passenger-bus service – that will take a slice out of its west boundary.

Millennium Boulevard is an urban promenade linking the plaza to Southern Park running along the eastern boundary of the park. Southern Park, also known as the Millennium Village Park, is the area where there's most to see at the moment, including some dramatic views of the Thames Barrier. The common or village green provides a focus for the new Millennium Village (phase 1 currently under construction, designed by Ralph Erskine), with space for sports and activities. The rest of the apartments

Richard Rogers Partnership/Devigne & Dalnoky/W S Atkins 1997

Richard Rogers Partnership/Devigne & Dalnoky/W S Atkins 1997

are designed around garden squares. A 3-hectare zone slopes towards the river incorporating two connected bodies of water totalling 0.7 hectare with 0.3 hectare of fringe reedbed and 0.5 hectare of damp grassland and shingle-mud fringe dedicated as habitats for water-based wildlife.

Riverside Walk is a 2.2-kilometre continuous 'leisure trail' for pedestrians and cyclists, forming a linear park (30–50 metres wide) along the eastern perimeter of the peninsula. At Quayside (adjacent to Millennium Plaza) there are stone steps, ramps and benches from which to enjoy the river, surrounded by a variety of ornamental grasses. Further south, Embankment Gardens are designed to echo the peninsula's original condition as an inter-tidal salt march and marsh grassland. Sheet-piled flood defences have been lowered to create a series of 7-metre-wide terraces – part lowered promenade, part river-based ecological terraces – for salt-marsh plant life and invertebrates. Exposure-tolerant species such as hornbeam and willow act as barriers.

The masterplan has been strongly criticised for not going far enough in terms of sustainability, especially where car transport is concerned. It's a shame that opportunities for sustainable urban drainage were missed. Everything looks as though it were thrown together at breakneck speed – it was, in time for the eve of a new Millennium.

ADDRESS Greenwich Peninsula, London SE10
CLIENT English Partnerships
LANDSCAPE CONSULTANTS Bernard Ede and Nicholas Pearson Associates
CIVIL ENGINEER W S Atkins TRANSPORT ENGINEER JMP
CONTRACT VALUE £ 147.5 million SIZE 119 hectares
TUBE Greenwich North RIVERBUS Greenwich
ACCESS open

Richard Rogers Partnership/Devigne & Dalnoky/W S Atkins 1997

Richard Rogers Partnership/Devigne & Dalnoky/W S Atkins 1997

Woolwich Park

The park was the subject of a limited competition in 1997. Several land-scape architects were invited to submit designs and local people voted the Whitelaw Turkington scheme their favourite. Certain comparisons can be made with Thames Barrier Park: both schemes involved reclamation of a derelict industrial site (in this case an old power-station coal yard) on the edge of the Thames; both are perceived as flagship projects that should act as the catalyst for urban regeneration of the local area. They have not, however, received comparable levels of publicity.

The park includes a generous grass amphitheatre, an egg-shaped kick-about area, and a securely fenced play area for small children (*à la* Helling Street, see page 6.2). Hoardings screen off the last land parcel to be acquired from the London Electricity Board and there is an application to the Sports Council for a grant to build a five-a-side football pitch.

The central feature is a broad 'slipway' with gently ramped steps that can double up as a series of platforms for exhibitions, events and the annual Greenwich and Docklands Art Festival. Tall timber river piles mounted on plinths (concealing powerpoints) frame views to the river. At night they form beacons whose quality of light changes with the level of the tide. The 2.5-metre flood-alleviation walls have been lowered to open up strong links between the river and Woolwich town centre. To satisfy flood-protection requirements, the whole park is built up as a series of revetments – a mixture of grass terraces and walls. To the west of the 'slipway', park trees are laid out in lines along the terraces.

Benches, flag lighting columns and railings are all purpose-designed and carefully positioned to provide spatial definition. The colour co-ordinated pinks and greys of the reconstituted concrete paviors, steps and bonded gravel are intentionally low-key – almost camouflage in this part of the world! Broadway Malayan's riverside walk and cycleway in regu-

Whitelaw Turkington 2000

Whitelaw Turkington 2000

lation green tarmac stands out in stark contrast, visually segregating the park from the river. Certain items are picked out in brighter colours within the park, such as the metal folly structures and play surfaces.

The park is daringly empty of clutter. It relies on the drama of the changing river and sky scenery which can sometimes be pretty desolate. Perhaps it's more realistic about its harsh urban environment than its more notorious neighbour – time will tell.

ADDRESS Woolwich High Street/Market Hill, London SE18
CLIENT Woolwich Development Agency in partnership with London Borough of Greenwich
CONSULTING ENGINEER Leuvin Fryer
CONTRACT VALUE £1.3 million
SIZE 2.7 hectares
RAIL Woolwich Dockyard
ACCESS open

Whitelaw Turkington 2000

Whitelaw Turkington 2000

index

Index

a guide to recent parks, gardens and urban spaces

a guide to recent parks, gardens and urban spaces

Index

a guide to recent parks, gardens and urban spaces

The photograph on page 3.9 is
reproduced by kind permission of Keith
Collie

The drawing on page 3.27 is reproduced
by kind permission of Allies and
Morrison

a guide to recent parks, gardens and urban spaces

London

A guide to recent architecture

As ever, a version of the development of London's economic, political and cultural life can be read in the new buildings going up all over the capital. After the excitement and farce of the city's millennium architecture (The London Eye, Peckham Library and Tate Modern on the one hand; the Dome and the infamous swaying Thames footbridge on the other), our rulers have built themselves one of the world's most lavish office blocks; two new skyscrapers are nearing completion at Canary Wharf – only recently among the capital's least-favoured properties, but now an astonishingly desirable address; industrial buildings are being renovated to house new-media firms and the people who own or work in them; and occasionally funding has been found for a school or public leisure facility. The city's decaying infrastructure has been boosted with the completion of the Jubilee Line extension. This fifth edition of *London: a guide to recent architecture* brings the picture up to date.

ISBN 1 84166 060 4
PRICE UK £10.00 US $15.00

Samantha Hardingham

Art London

A guide

As the London art scene consolidates its position as world leader, *Art London* is the first comprehensive guide to the venues that make the capital tick. From the artist-run or alternative spaces of the East End to the blue-chip showrooms of the West End, and beyond, it is a vibrant and opinionated tour of spaces for contemporary art, encompassing the key personalities and most exciting exhibitions of the last few years.

With descriptions and illustrations of more than sixty venues for contemporary art, divided into geographical sections, this is the definitive guide for the curious and the connoisseur alike.

ISBN 1 84166 050 7
PRICE UK £10.00 US $15.00

Martin Coomer

London Walking
A handbook for survival

More than you could have imagined you needed to know to walk London, with vital advice to consider before you cross a road, *London Walking* is both practical guide and pointer to new possibilities.

The book includes useful discourse on subjects such as 'What is traffic?', how to recognise the kerb, and walking inside buildings; historical background on the Tufty Club and how to walk to escape the plague; more than 70 helpful illustrations; and an exercise in how far you can walk in a day following the sun. Armed with these appropriate strategies and techniques, it becomes possible to experience the city at its haptic, hectic best.

London Walking is a handbook for survival. Hard fact lies alongside personal commentary. Don't set foot on the pavement without it.

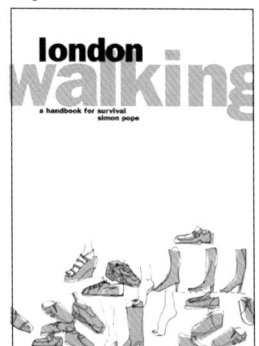

ISBN 1 84166 056 6
PRICE UK £10.00 US $15.00

Simon Pope